Constructing a
Life Philosophy

OPPOSING VIEWPOINTS®

Other Books of Related Interest

Constructing a
Life Philosophy

O P P O S I N G   V I E W P O I N T S ®

Mark Ray Schmidt, Ph.D.,
University of Arkansas at Monticello, *Book Editor*

Daniel Leone, *President*
Bonnie Szumski, *Publisher*
Scott Barbour, *Managing Editor*
Bruno Leone, *Series Editor*

OPPOSING
VIEWPOINTS®
SERIES

Greenhaven Press, Inc., San Diego, California

Cover photo: Photodisc

Library of Congress Cataloging-in-Publication Data

Constructing a life philosophy : opposing viewpoints / Mark Ray
  Schmidt, book editor.
    p. cm. — (Opposing viewpoints series)
    Includes bibliographical references and index.
    ISBN 0-7377-1263-5 (pbk. : alk. paper)
  ISBN 0-7377-1264-3 (alk. paper)
    1. Life. I. Schmidt, Mark Ray, 1953–   II. Opposing
viewpoints series (Unnumbered)

BD431 .C664 2002
100—dc21   2001033501
                                                         CIP

Greenhaven Press, Inc.
10911 Technology Place, San Diego, CA 92127

"Congress shall make
no law...abridging the
freedom of speech, or of
the press."

First Amendment to the U.S. Constitution

The basic foundation of our democracy is the First
Amendment guarantee of freedom of expression.
The Opposing Viewpoints Series is dedicated to the
concept of this basic freedom and the idea that it is
more important to practice it than to enshrine it.

Contents

Why Consider Opposing Viewpoints?

"The only way in which a human being can make some approach to knowing the whole of a subject is by hearing what can be said about it by persons of every variety of opinion and studying all modes in which it can be looked at by every character of mind. No wise man ever acquired his wisdom in any mode but this."

John Stuart Mill

In our media-intensive culture it is not difficult to find differing opinions. Thousands of newspapers and magazines and dozens of radio and television talk shows resound with differing points of view. The difficulty lies in deciding which opinion to agree with and which "experts" seem the most credible. The more inundated we become with differing opinions and claims, the more essential it is to hone critical reading and thinking skills to evaluate these ideas. Opposing Viewpoints books address this problem directly by presenting stimulating debates that can be used to enhance and teach these skills. The varied opinions contained in each book examine many different aspects of a single issue. While examining these conveniently edited opposing views, readers can develop critical thinking skills such as the ability to compare and contrast authors' credibility, facts, argumentation styles, use of persuasive techniques, and other stylistic tools. In short, the Opposing Viewpoints Series is an ideal way to attain the higher-level thinking and reading skills so essential in a culture of diverse and contradictory opinions.

In addition to providing a tool for critical thinking, Opposing Viewpoints books challenge readers to question their own strongly held opinions and assumptions. Most people form their opinions on the basis of upbringing, peer pressure, and personal, cultural, or professional bias. By reading carefully balanced opposing views, readers must directly confront new ideas as well as the opinions of those with whom they disagree. This is not to simplistically argue that everyone who reads opposing views will—or should—change his or her opinion. Instead, the series enhances readers' understanding of their own views by encouraging confrontation with opposing ideas. Careful examination of others' views can lead to the readers' understanding of the logical inconsistencies in their own opinions, perspective on why they hold an opinion, and the consideration of the possibility that their opinion requires further evaluation.

Evaluating Other Opinions

To ensure that this type of examination occurs, Opposing Viewpoints books present all types of opinions. Prominent spokespeople on different sides of each issue as well as well-known professionals from many disciplines challenge the reader. An additional goal of the series is to provide a forum for other, less known, or even unpopular viewpoints. The opinion of an ordinary person who has had to make the decision to cut off life support from a terminally ill relative, for example, may be just as valuable and provide just as much insight as a medical ethicist's professional opinion. The editors have two additional purposes in including these less known views. One, the editors encourage readers to respect others' opinions—even when not enhanced by professional credibility. It is only by reading or listening to and objectively evaluating others' ideas that one can determine whether they are worthy of consideration. Two, the inclusion of such viewpoints encourages the important critical thinking skill of objectively evaluating an author's credentials and bias. This evaluation will illuminate an author's reasons for taking a particular stance on an issue and will aid in readers' evaluation of the author's ideas.

It is our hope that these books will give readers a deeper understanding of the issues debated and an appreciation of the complexity of even seemingly simple issues when good and honest people disagree. This awareness is particularly important in a democratic society such as ours in which people enter into public debate to determine the common good. Those with whom one disagrees should not be regarded as enemies but rather as people whose views deserve careful examination and may shed light on one's own.

Thomas Jefferson once said that "difference of opinion leads to inquiry, and inquiry to truth." Jefferson, a broadly educated man, argued that "if a nation expects to be ignorant and free . . . it expects what never was and never will be." As individuals and as a nation, it is imperative that we consider the opinions of others and examine them with skill and discernment. The Opposing Viewpoints Series is intended to help readers achieve this goal.

David L. Bender and Bruno Leone,
Founders

Greenhaven Press anthologies primarily consist of previously published material taken from a variety of sources, including periodicals, books, scholarly journals, newspapers, government documents, and position papers from private and public organizations. These original sources are often edited for length and to ensure their accessibility for a young adult audience. The anthology editors also change the original titles of these works in order to clearly present the main thesis of each viewpoint and to explicitly indicate the opinion presented in the viewpoint. These alterations are made in consideration of both the reading and comprehension levels of a young adult audience. Every effort is made to ensure that Greenhaven Press accurately reflects the original intent of the authors included in this anthology.

Introduction

A book like this is published to meet many needs. However, three goals were dominant in the creation of this work: (1) to satisfy the reader's curiosity about philosophy, religion, and morals; (2) to assist the reader who is developing his or her personal conclusions about the meaning of life and about the goals which he or she will strive toward; (3) to assist the reader in better understanding the values, religious ideas, and personal goals of other people.

Curiosity is a wonderful part of being a human. It is the force which makes us instinctive explorers. Just as peoples such as the Greeks and the Vikings explored their physical world, we explore our personal world by studying history, psychology, biology, political science, and physics. Just as Europeans were curious about finding an ocean route to India and China at the time of Columbus, we are explorers of ideas when we go to the library for books, learn a new computer program, or surf the internet. This book will hopefully assist you as you explore the disciplines of philosophy, religion, and ethics. It is in these disciplines that people have asked the most searching questions about life's meaning and the values which should guide them.

There is a second reason to read this book; we occasionally have times when we ask ourselves: What do I really believe? What do I want to do in my life? What religious and moral principles should guide me? These questions are quite common in all cultures, in all historical periods. When we ask such questions, we are seeking a way to unify our lives around a philosophical principle, a religious belief, or a moral absolute. This book will give you a few of the ways these seminal questions have been answered by others. Though this book cannot fully explain the many religious and philosophical points of view available, it does serve as a catalyst for further study and reflection.

Whether or not we are building our personal philosophy of life, we need to consider the third reason to read this collection of viewpoints. We need to understand other people. This book is an excellent tool for gaining a greater awareness of the beliefs held by others. All of us need a general understanding of the goals, religious beliefs, moral priorities, and philosophical views held by others. Only then can we understand our neighbors—whether they are distant peoples or the person next door.

As we survey the history of humanity, we find that the enthusiasm with which people have explored their physical world is comparable to their zeal for journeying into the world of ideas. Humans have continually asked about the meaning of life and sought the best ways to live socially and privately. As social beings, humans are continually brought in contact with others who hold differing systems of beliefs. Hopefully, this book will spark your curiosity, helping you better understand not only yourself but others as well.

CHAPTER 1

The Importance of Choosing a Life Philosophy

Chapter Preface

When we think about the great problems facing humanity, our attention automatically turns to such issues as poverty, warfare, pollution, and disease. While these problems are clearly important and urgent, there are other problems which are equally urgent, but often overlooked. This chapter illustrates how and why some of the most crucial issues of our lives often go unnoticed.

In the first viewpoint, M. Scott Peck, a contemporary psychiatrist, explains that we need a "map" to find our way through life. What Peck is referring to is our basic beliefs which guide our daily decisions through the twists and turns of life. The problem is that our maps are often inaccurate. Peck points out that we need to adjust our maps—our understanding of how life works—according to the reality of our lives. Too often we are self-deceptive. We refuse to honestly examine our lives and our problems. Peck concludes that this dishonesty can greatly hinder us.

In the second viewpoint, the ancient philosopher Plato presents his famous story of the cave. Like Peck, Plato is concerned that most of us are confused in our understanding of the world and ourselves. Plato suggests that we are trapped by our immediate, first impressions of things. We need to use our reasoning abilities to escape from this trap and to find a more accurate understanding of ourselves and our world.

In the third viewpoint, Sam Keen and Anne Valley-Fox explain that we need a "myth" to explain our lives. Their use of the term myth is very similar to Peck's concept of a map which guides our lives. Keen and Valley-Fox challenge us to consider the myths (the dominating story-lines) which guide our culture, our families, and our individual lives. Only as we come to understand the role of myth in our lives today, will we be able to make the necessary adjustments which both Peck and Plato challenge us to make in our lives.

These authors agree that confused thinking and self-deception are two of our greatest enemies. The authors also agree that we must resist the temptation of accepting the world around us at simple face value. We must seek truth. To do this, we must be prepared to examine our most basic assumptions.

> *"Our view of reality is like a map with which to negotiate the terrain of life. If the map is true and accurate, we will generally know where we are."*

Choosing a Map for Life

M. Scott Peck

M. Scott Peck became famous when he published *The Road Less Traveled* in 1978. In this book, Peck uses his experiences as a psychiatrist to argue that people need to face the difficulties of life and overcome them with honesty, commitment, and spiritual growth. Since then, Peck has published more than fourteen books on similar themes. In the following viewpoint, Peck challenges his readers to examine how they view the world and how they view themselves. If people do not honestly face the world and themselves, their lives will, at best, be limited. Peck warns that dishonesty with ourselves can often do great harm.

As you read, consider the following questions:
1. According to Peck, why are "maps" important in our lives?
2. Why is it difficult to update our maps of the world?
3. Why are self-discipline and truth so important to Peck?

Truth is reality. That which is false is unreal. The more clearly we see the reality of the world, the better equipped we are to deal with the world. The less clearly we see the reality of the world—the more our minds are befuddled by falsehood, misperceptions and illusions—the less able we will be to determine correct courses of action and make wise decisions.

Map of Life

Our view of reality is like a map with which to negotiate the terrain of life. If the map is true and accurate, we will generally know where we are, and if we have decided where we want to go, we will generally know how to get there. If the map is false and inaccurate, we generally will be lost.

While this is obvious, it is something that most people to a greater or lesser degree choose to ignore. They ignore it because our route to reality is not easy. First of all, we are not born with maps; we have to make them, and the making requires effort. The more effort we make to appreciate and perceive reality, the larger and more accurate our maps will be. But many do not want to make this effort. Some stop making it by the end of adolescence. Their maps are small and sketchy, their views of the world narrow and misleading. By the end of middle age most people have given up the effort. They feel certain that their maps are complete and their Weltanschauung [world-view, or assumptions] is correct (indeed, even sacrosanct), and they are no longer interested in new information. It is as if they are tired. Only a relative and fortunate few continue until the moment of death exploring the mystery of reality, ever enlarging and refining and redefining their understanding of the world and what is true.

Revising Life's Map

But the biggest problem of map-making is not that we have to start from scratch, but that if our maps are to be accurate we have to continually revise them. The world itself is constantly changing. Glaciers come, glaciers go. Cultures come, cultures go. There is too little technology, there is too much technology. Even more dramatically, the vantage point from which we view the world is constantly and quite rapidly changing. When we are children we are dependent, power-less. As adults we may be powerful. Yet in illness or an infirm old age we may become powerless and dependent again. When we have children to care for, the world looks different from when we have none; when we are raising infants, the world seems different from when we are raising adolescents. When we are poor, the world looks different from when we are rich. We are daily bombarded with new information as to the nature of reality. If we are to incorporate this infor-mation, we must continually revise our maps, and sometimes when enough new information has accumulated, we must make very major revisions. The process of making revisions, particularly major revisions, is painful, sometimes excruciat-ingly painful. And herein lies the major source of many of the ills of mankind.

What happens when one has striven long and hard to de-velop a working view of the world, a seemingly useful, workable map, and then is confronted with new informa-tion suggesting that that view is wrong and the map needs to be largely redrawn? The painful effort required seems frightening, almost overwhelming. What we do more often than not, and usually unconsciously, is to ignore the new in-formation. Often this act of ignoring is much more than passive. We may denounce the new information as false, dangerous, heretical, the work of the devil. We may actually crusade against it, and even attempt to manipulate the world so as to make it conform to our view of reality. Rather than try to change the map, an individual may try to destroy the new reality. Sadly, such a person may expend much more energy ultimately in defending an outmoded view of the world than would have been required to revise and cor-rect it in the first place.

This process of active clinging to an outmoded view of reality is the basis for much mental illness. Psychiatrists re-fer to it as transference. There are probably as many subtle variations of the definition of transference as there are psy-chiatrists. My own definition is: Transference is that set of ways of perceiving and responding to the world which is developed in childhood and which is usually entirely ap-propriate to the childhood environment (indeed, often life-saving) but which is *inappropriately* transferred into the adult environment.

Examples of Transference

The ways in which transference manifests itself, while always pervasive and destructive, are often subtle. Yet the clearest examples must be unsubtle. One such example was a patient whose treatment failed by virtue of his transference. He was a brilliant but unsuccessful computer technician in his early thirties, who came to see me because his wife had left him, taking their two children. He was not particularly unhappy to lose her, but he was devastated by the loss of his children, to whom he was deeply attached. It was in the hope of regaining them that he initiated psychotherapy, since his wife firmly stated she would never return to him unless he had psychiatric treatment. Her principal complaints about him were that he was continually and irrationally jealous of her, and yet at the same time aloof from her, cold, distant, uncommunicative and unaffectionate. She also complained of his frequent changes of employment. His life since adolescence had been markedly unstable. During adolescence he was involved in frequent minor altercations with the police, and had been jailed three times for intoxication, belligerence, "loitering," and "interfering with the duties of an officer." He dropped out of college, where he was studying electrical engineering, because, as he said, "My teachers were a bunch of hypocrites, hardly different from the police." Because of his brilliance and creativeness in the field of computer technology, his services were in high demand by industry. But he had never been able to advance or keep a job for more than a year and a half, occasionally being fired, more often quitting after disputes with his supervisors, whom he described as "liars and cheats, interested only in protecting their own ass." His most frequent expression was "You can't trust a goddam soul." He described his childhood as "normal" and his parents as "average." In the brief period of time he spent with me, however, he casually and unemotionally recounted numerous instances during childhood in which his parents had let him down. They promised him a bike for his birthday, but they forgot about it and gave him something else. Once they forgot his birthday entirely, but he saw nothing drastically wrong with this since "they were very busy." They would promise to do things with him on weekends, but then were usually "too busy." Numerous times they forgot to pick him up from meetings or parties because "they had a lot on their minds."

What happened to this man was that when he was a young child he suffered painful disappointment after painful disappointment through his parents' lack of caring. Gradually or suddenly—I don't know which—he came to the agonizing realization in mid-childhood that he could not trust his parents. Once he realized this, however, he began to feel better, and his life became more comfortable. He no longer expected things from his parents or got his hopes up when they made promises. When he stopped trusting his parents the frequency and severity of his disappointments diminished dramatically.

The Need for a Life Plan

Anyone who has read Plato's account of the trial of Socrates will remember his observation that an unexamined life is not worth living. When we understand what he means, I think we will also be led to conclude that an unplanned life cannot be lived well. That conclusion directs the effort of this book to answer the question with which it is concerned, for it tells us in advance what we are looking for—*a sound and practical plan of life that will help us to make our whole life good.*

Mortimer J. Adler, *The Time of Our Lives*, 1970.

Such an adjustment, however, is the basis for future problems. To a child his or her parents are everything; they represent the world. The child does not have the perspective to see that other parents are different and frequently better. He assumes that the way his parents do things is the way that things are done. Consequently the realization—the "reality"—that this child came to was not "I can't trust my parents" but "I can't trust people." Not trusting people therefore became the map with which he entered adolescence and adulthood. With this map and with an abundant store of resentment resulting from his many disappointments, it was inevitable that he came into conflict with authority figures—police, teachers, employers. And these conflicts only served to reinforce his feeling that people who had anything to give him in the world couldn't be trusted. He had many opportunities to revise his map, but they were all passed up. For one thing, the only way he could learn that there were some people in the adult world he could trust would be to risk trusting them, and that would require a deviation from his map to begin with. For another, such relearning would require him to revise his view of his parents—to realize that they did not love him, that he did not have a normal childhood and that his parents were not average in their callousness to his needs. Such a realization would have been extremely painful. Finally, because his distrust of people was a realistic adjustment to the reality of his childhood, it was an adjustment that worked in terms of diminishing his pain and suffering. Since it is extremely difficult to give up an adjustment that once worked so well, he continued his course of distrust, unconsciously creating situations that served to reinforce it, alienating himself from everyone, making it impossible for himself to enjoy love, warmth, intimacy and affection. He could not even allow himself closeness with his wife; she, too, could not be trusted. The only people he could relate with intimately were his two children. They were the only ones over whom he had control, the only ones who had no authority over him, the only ones he could trust in the whole world.

When problems of transference are involved, as they usually are, psychotherapy is, among other things, a process of map-revising. Patients come to therapy because their maps are clearly not working. But how they may cling to them and fight the process every step of the way! Frequently their need to cling to their maps and fight against losing them is so great that therapy becomes impossible. . . .

Truth Can Overcome Transference

The problem of transference is not simply a problem between parents and children, husbands and wives, employers and employees, between friends, between groups, and even between nations. It is interesting to speculate, for instance, on the role that transference issues play in international affairs. Our national leaders are human beings who all had childhoods and childhood experiences that shaped them. What map was Hitler following, and where did it come from? What map were American leaders following in initiating, executing and maintaining the war in Vietnam? Clearly it was a map very different from that of the generation that succeeded theirs. In what ways did the national experience of the Depression years contribute to their map, and the experience of the fifties and sixties contribute to the map of the younger generation? If the national experience of the thirties and forties contributed to the behavior of American leaders in waging war in Vietnam, how appropriate was that experience to the realities of the sixties and seventies? How can we revise our maps more rapidly?

Truth or reality is avoided when it is painful. We can revise our maps only when we have the discipline to overcome that pain. To have such discipline, we must be totally dedicated to truth. That is to say that we must always hold truth, as best we can determine it, to be more important, more vital to our self-interest, than our comfort. Conversely, we must always consider our personal discomfort relatively unimportant and, indeed, even welcome it in the service of the search for truth. Mental health is an ongoing process of dedication to reality at all costs.

What does a life of total dedication to the truth mean? It means, first of all, a life of continuous and never-ending stringent self-examination. We know the world only through our relationship to it. Therefore, to know the world, we must not only examine it but we must simultaneously examine the examiner. . . .

Examination of the world without is never as personally painful as examination of the world within, and it is certainly because of the pain involved in a life of genuine self-examination that the majority steer away from it. Yet when one is dedicated to the truth this pain seems relatively unimportant—and less and less important (and therefore less and less painful) the farther one proceeds on the path of self-examination.

A life of total dedication to the truth also means a life of willingness to be personally challenged. The only way that we can be certain that our map of reality is valid is to expose it to the criticism and challenge of other map-makers. Otherwise we live in a closed system—within a bell jar, to use Sylvia Plath's analogy, rebreathing only our own fetid air, more and more subject to delusion. Yet, because of the pain inherent in the process of revising our map of reality, we mostly seek to avoid or ward off any challenges to its validity. To our children we say, "Don't talk back to me, I'm your parent." To our spouse we give the message, "Let's live and let live. If you criticize me, I'll be a bitch to live with, and you'll regret it." To their families and the world the elderly give the message, "I am old and fragile. If you challenge me I may die or at least you will bear upon your head the responsibility for making my last days on earth miserable." To our employees we communicate, "If you are bold enough to challenge me at all, you had best do so very circumspectly indeed or else you'll find yourself looking for another job."

The tendency to avoid challenge is so omnipresent in human beings that it can properly be considered a characteristic of human nature. But calling it natural does not mean it is essential or beneficial or unchangeable behavior. It is also natural to defecate in our pants and never brush our teeth. Yet we teach ourselves to do the unnatural until the unnatural becomes itself second nature. Indeed, all self-discipline might be defined as teaching ourselves to do the unnatural. . . .

For individuals and organizations to be open to challenge, it is necessary that their maps of reality be *truly* open for inspection. . . . It means a continuous and never-ending process of self-monitoring to assure that our communications—not only the words that we say but also the way we say them—invariably reflect as accurately as humanly possible the truth or reality as we know it.

Such honesty does not come painlessly. The reason people lie is to avoid the pain of challenge and its consequences. . . .

We lie, of course, not only to others but also to ourselves. The challenges to our adjustment—our maps—from our own consciences and our own realistic perceptions may be every bit as legitimate and painful as any challenge from the public . . . which is why most people opt for a life of very limited honesty and openness and relative closedness, hiding themselves and their maps from the world. It is easier that way. Yet the rewards of the difficult life of honesty and dedication to the truth are more than commensurate with the demands. By virtue of the fact that their maps are continually being challenged, open people are continually growing people.

"Imagine mankind as dwelling in an underground cave."

Are We Living in a Cave?

Plato

Plato (427–347 B.C.) lived and taught philosophy in ancient Athens. In the following viewpoint, Plato asks his audience to imagine prisoners living in a cave. The people face a wall where shadows of various objects dance back and forth. The prisoners cannot turn their heads to discover the true nature of the shadows. Further, the prisoners cannot leave the cave to discover what the reality creating the shadows is like. Plato uses this story to illustrate his belief that we are trapped by our imperfect, subjective impressions of the world. Plato believes that people too quickly accept the first appearance of things. What people experience as reality is really a distorted reflection, or shadow, of the true reality. Plato believed that humans (in the present life) will never completely understand the world. Thus, Plato challenges his listeners to carefully use reason as a tool to examine all their beliefs.

As you read, consider the following questions:
1. According to Plato, humans sometimes find it hard to face reality. Why is this?
2. What is the nature of personal growth and education? Is Plato correct in suggesting that teachers often need to push students in order for them to face the truth?
3. What does Plato tell us about first impressions and prejudice?

Excerpted from *The Republic*, by Plato, in *The Great Dialogues of Plato*, edited by Eric H. Warmington and Philip G. Rouse, translated by W.H.D. Rouse (New York: New American Library, 1956).

"Next, then," I said, "take the following parable of education and ignorance as a picture of the condition of our nature. Imagine mankind as dwelling in an underground cave with a long entrance open to the light across the whole width of the cave; in this they have been from childhood, with necks and legs fettered, so they have to stay where they are. They cannot move their heads round because of the fetters, and they can only look forward, but light comes to them from fire burning behind them higher up at a distance. Between the fire and the prisoners is a road above their level, and along it imagine a low wall has been built, as puppet showmen have screens in front of their people over which they work their puppets." "I see," he said.

The Bearers and Things Carried

"See, then, bearers carrying along this wall all sorts of articles which they hold projecting above the wall, statues of men and other living things,[1] made of stone or wood and all kinds of stuff, some of the bearers speaking and some silent, as you might expect."

"What a remarkable, image," he said, "and what remarkable prisoners!"

"Just like ourselves," I said. "For, first of all, tell me this: What do you think such people would have seen of themselves and each other except their shadows, which the fire cast on the opposite wall of the cave?"

"I don't see how they could see anything else," said he, "if they were compelled to keep their heads unmoving all their lives!"

"Very well, what of the things being carried along? Would not this be the same?"

"Of course it would."

"Suppose the prisoners were able to talk together, don't you think that when they named the shadows which they saw passing they would believe they were naming things?[2]

"Necessarily."

"Then if their prison had an echo from the opposite wall,

1. Including models of trees, etc. 2. Which they had never seen. They would say "tree" when it was only a shadow of the model of a tree.

27

whenever one of the passing bearers uttered a sound, would they not suppose that the passing shadow must be making the sound? Don't you think so?"

"Indeed I do," he said.

"If so," said I, "such persons would certainly believe that there were no realities except those shadows of hand-made things."[3]

"So it must be," said he.

Removal of the Fetters

"Now consider," said I, "what their release would be like, and their cure from these fetters and their folly; let us imagine whether it might naturally be something like this. One might be released, and compelled suddenly to stand up and turn his neck round, and to walk and look towards the firelight; all this would hurt him, and he would be too much dazzled to see distinctly those things whose shadows he had seen before. What do you think he would say, if someone told him that what he saw before was foolery, but now he saw more rightly, being a bit nearer reality, and turned towards what was a little more real? What if he were shown each of the passing things, and compelled by questions to answer what each one was? Don't you think he would be puzzled, and believe what he saw before was more true than what was shown to him now?"

"Far more," he said.

"Then suppose he were compelled to look towards the real light, it would hurt his eyes, and he would escape by turning them away to the things which he was able to look at, and these he would believe to be clearer than what was being shown to him."

"Just so," said he.

Leaving the Cave

"Suppose, now," said I, "that someone should drag him thence by force, up the rough ascent, the steep way up, and never stop until he could drag him out into the light of the sun, would he not be distressed and furious at being dragged;

3. Shadows of artificial things, not even the shadow of a growing tree: another stage from reality.

and when he came into the light, the brilliance would fill his eyes and he would not be able to see even one of the things now called real?"[4]

"That he would not," said he, "all of a sudden."

"He would have to get used to it, surely, I think, if he is to see the things above. First he would most easily look at shadows, after that images of mankind and the rest in water, lastly the things themselves. After this he would find it easier to survey by night the heavens themselves and all that is in them, gazing at the light of the stars and moon, rather than by day the sun and the sun's light."

"Of course."

"Last of all, I suppose, the sun; he could look on the sun itself by itself in its own place, and see what it is like, not reflections of it in water or as it appears in some alien setting."

"Necessarily," said he.

The Cave

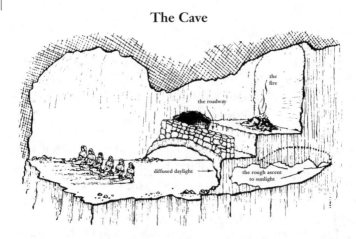

The Great Dialogues of Plato, Warmington and Rouse, eds.

"And only after all this he might reason about it, how this is he who provides seasons and years, and is set over all there is in the visible region, and he is in a manner the cause of all things which they saw."

"Yes, it is clear," said he, "that after all that, he would come to this last."

4. To the next stage of knowledge: the real thing, not the artificial puppet.

"Very good. Let him be reminded of his first habitation, and what was wisdom in that place, and of his fellow-prisoners there; don't you think he would bless himself for the change, and pity them?"

"Yes, indeed."

"And if there were honours and praises among them and prizes for the one who saw the passing things most sharply and remembered best which of them used to come before and which after and which together, and from these was best able to prophesy accordingly what was going to come—do you believe he would set his desire on that, and envy those who were honoured men or potentates among them? Would he not feel as Homer says,[5] and heartily desire rather to be serf of some landless man on earth and to endure anything in the world, rather than to opine as they did and to live in that way?"

"Yes, indeed," said he, "he would rather accept anything than live like that."

Returning to the Cave

"Then again," I said, "just consider; if such a one should go down again and sit on his old seat, would he not get his eyes full of darkness coming in suddenly out of the sun?"

"Very much so," said he.

"And if he should have to compete with those who had been always prisoners, by laying down the law about those shadows while he was blinking before his eyes were settled down—and it would take a good long time to get used to things—wouldn't they all laugh at him and say he had spoiled his eyesight by going up there, and it was not worthwhile so much as to try to go up? And would they not kill anyone who tried to release them and take them up, if they could somehow lay hands on him and kill him?"[6]

"That they would!" said he.

Conclusion

"Then we must apply this image, my dear Glaucon," said I, "to all we have been saying. The world of our sight is like the

5. *Odyssey* xi   6. Plato probably alludes to the death of Socrates. See *Apology*.

habitation in prison, the firelight there to the sunlight here, the ascent and the view of the upper world is the rising of the soul into the world of mind; put it so and you will not be far from my own surmise, since that is what you want to hear; but God knows if it is really true. At least, what appears to me is, that in the world of known, last of all,[7] is the idea of the good, and with what toil to be seen! And seen, this must be inferred to be the cause of all right and beautiful things for all, which gives birth to light and the king of light in the world of sight, and, in the world of mind, herself the queen produces truth and reason; and she must be seen by one who is to act with reason publicly or privately."

7. The end of our search

> *"We gain personal authority and power in the measure that we . . . discover and create a personal myth that illuminates and informs us."*

Discovering Our Personal Myth

Sam Keen and Anne Valley-Fox

Sam Keen and Anne Valley-Fox are students of philosophy, religion, and myth. They are not concerned with ancient myths, but with the stories people create today to explain their experiences. For example, in one book (*The Faces of the Enemy*), Keen explains how individuals and nations create negative images of their enemies to justify their conflict with their enemies. This viewpoint is taken from *Your Mythic Journey*. The authors explain that all humans need a "story line," or a myth, which puts life together into a meaningful whole.

As you read, consider the following questions:
1. How do the authors define myth? How do other people use this term?
2. What do the authors mean when they say that myths are like an iceberg?
3. Do myths function the same way for nations, families, and individuals?

It seems that Americans are finally taking seriously what Carl Jung, this Swiss psychologist, said is the most important question we can ask ourselves: "What myth are we living?". . .

What Is a Myth?

What is a myth? Few words have been subject to as much abuse and been as ill-defined as *myth*. Journalists usually use it to mean a "lie," "fabrication," "illusion," "mistake," or something similar. It is the opposite of what is supposedly a "fact," of what is "objectively" the case, and of what is "reality." In this usage myth is at best a silly story and at worst a cynical untruth. Theologians and propagandists often use myth as a way of characterizing religious beliefs and ideologies other than their own.

Such trivialization of the notion of myth reflects false certainties of dogmatic minds, an ignorance of the mythic assumptions that underlie the commonly accepted view of "reality," and a refusal to consider how much our individual and communal lives are shaped by dramatic scenarios and "historical" narratives that are replete with accounts of the struggle between good and evil empires: our godly heroes versus the demonic enemy.

In a strict sense *myth* refers to "an intricate set of interlocking stories, rituals, rites, and customs that inform and give the pivotal sense of meaning and direction to a person, family, community, or culture." A living myth, like an iceberg, is 10 percent visible and 90 percent beneath the surface of consciousness. While it involves a conscious celebration of certain values, which are always personified in a pantheon of heroes (from the wily Ulysses to the managing Lee Iacocca) and villains (from the betraying Judas to the barbarous Moammar Kadafi), it also includes the unspoken consensus, the habitual way of seeing things, the unquestioned assumptions, the automatic stance. It is differing cultural myths that make cows sacred objects for Hindus and hamburgers meals for Methodists, or turn dogs into pets for Americans and roasted delicacies for the Chinese.

At least 51 percent of the people in a society are not self-consciously aware of the myth that informs their existence. Cultural consensus is created by an unconscious conspiracy to consider the myth "the truth," "the way things *really* are." In other words, a majority is made up of literalists, men and women who are not critical or reflective about the guiding "truths"—myths—of their own group. To a tourist in a strange land, an anthropologist studying a tribe, or a psychologist observing a patient, the myth is obvious. But to the person who lives within the mythic horizon, it is nearly invisible.

For instance, most Americans would consider potlatch feasts, in which Northwest Indian tribes systematically destroy their wealth, to be irrational and mythic but would consider the habit of browsing in malls and buying expensive things we do not need (conspicuous consumption) to be a perfectly reasonable way to spend a Saturday afternoon. To most Americans the Moslem notion of *jihad*—holy war—is a dangerous myth. But our struggle against "atheistic communism" is a righteous duty. Ask a born-again Christian about the myth of the atonement, and you will be told it is no myth at all but a revealed truth. Ask a true believer of Marxism about the myth of the withering away of the state, and you will get a long explanation about the "scientific" laws of the dialectic of history.

What Is a Myth?

I use myth to mean the systematic, unconscious way of structuring reality that governs a culture as a whole, or a people, or a tribe. It can govern a corporation, a family, or a person. It's the underlying story.

Sam Keen in *A World of Ideas II*, 1990.

I suggest two analogies that may help to counteract the popular trivialized notion of myth. The dominant myth that informs a person or a culture is like the "information" contained in DNA or the program in the systems disk of a computer. Myth is the software, the cultural DNA, the unconscious information, the metaprogram that governs the way we see "reality" and the way we behave.

Myths Can Be Creative or Destructive

The organizing myth of any culture functions in ways that may be either creative or destructive, healthful or pathological. By providing a world picture and a set of stories that explain why things are as they are, it creates consensus, sanctifies the social order, and gives the individual an authorized map of the path of life. A myth creates the plotline that organizes the diverse experiences of a person or a community into a single story.

The Importance of Stories

In a world of fluctuating material possessions, stories provide psychic possessions, representing one aspect of life over which one has control. The story belongs to the individual, providing a means of achieving stability and equilibrium.

Telling a story organizes an individual's impressions of experience. Consider the impulse to bear witness, which characterizes and motivates survivors of devastating events and personal tragedies. The urge to speak out about the tragedy helps the survivor extract significance from absurdity and meaning from meaninglessness. Without the story, there is nothing on which to stand, no context from which to organize meaning. By telling the story, one organizes meaning in a way that makes it possible to cope with what happened. This organization does not imply understanding. People who survived Hiroshima, Nagasaki, the Holocaust, and Vietnam may never understand why the events took place, but they are able to organize what happened to them in a way that helps them cope.

Catherine Sullivan Norton, *Life Metaphors*, 1989.

But in the same measure that myth gives us security and identity, it also creates selective blindness, narrowness, and rigidity because it is intrinsically conservative. It encourages us to follow the faith of our fathers, to hold to the time-honored truths, to imitate the way of the heroes, to repeat the formulas and rituals in exactly the same way they were done in the good old days. As long as no radical change is necessary for survival, the status quo remains sacred, the myth and ritual are unquestioned, and the patterns of life, like the seasons of the year, repeat themselves. But when crisis comes—a natural catastrophe, a military defeat, the introduction of a new technology—the mythic mind is at a loss to deal with novelty. As Marshall McLuhan said, it tries to "walk into the future looking through a rearview mirror."

Families Have Myths

Every family, like a miniculture, also has an elaborate system of stories and rituals that differentiate it from other families. The Murphys, being Irish, understand full well that Uncle Paddy is a bit of a rogue and drinks a tad too much. The Cohens, being Jewish, are haunted each year at Passover when they remember the family that perished in the Holocaust. The Keens, being Calvinists, are predestined to be slightly more righteous and right than others, even when they are wrong. And within the family each member's place is defined by a series of stories. Obedient to the family script, Jane, "who always was very motherly even as a little girl," married young and had children immediately, while Pat, "who was a wild one and not cut out for marriage," sowed oat after oat before finding fertile ground.

Family myths, like those of the Kennedy clan, may give us an impulse to strive for excellence and a sense of pride that helps us endure hardship and tragedy. Or they may, like the myths of alcoholic or abusive families, pass a burden of guilt, shame, and failure from generation to generation as abused children, in turn, become abusive parents, ad nauseam. The sins, virtues, and myths of the fathers are passed on to the children of future generations.

Every Individual Has a Personal Myth

Finally, the entire legacy and burden of cultural and family myth comes to rest on the individual. Each person is a repository of stories. To the degree that any one of us reaches toward autonomy, we must begin a process of sorting through the trash and treasures we have been given, keeping some and rejecting others. We gain the full dignity and power of our persons only when we create a narrative account of our lives, dramatize our existence, and forge a coherent personal myth that combines elements of our cultural myth and family myth with unique stories that come from our experience. As my friend David Steere once pointed out to me, the common root of "authority" and "authorship" tells us a great deal about power. Whoever authors your story authorizes your actions. We gain personal authority and power in the measure that we question the myth that is upheld by "the authorities" and discover and create a personal myth that illuminates and informs us.

What George Santayana said about cultures is equally true for individuals: "Those who do not remember history are condemned to repeat it." If we do not make the effort to become conscious of our personal myths gradually, we become dominated by what psychologists have variously called repetition compulsion, autonomous complexes, engrams, routines, scripts, games. One fruitful way to think of neurosis is to consider it a tape loop, an oft-told story that we repeat in our inner dialogues with ourselves and with others. "Well, I'm just not the kind of person who can . . ." "I never could . . ." "I wouldn't think of . . .". While personal myths give us a sense of identity, continuity and security, they become constricting and boring if they are not revised from time to time. To remain vibrant throughout a lifetime we must always be inventing ourselves, weaving new themes into our life-narratives, remembering our past, re-visioning our future, reauthorizing the myth by which we live.

What Gives Life Ultimate Meaning?

Chapter Preface

Imagine walking into a school or office and seeing a new, unusual type of computer. We might logically ask, "What is it for?" If we see workers clearing land and beginning to build a metal structure, we would probably inquire, "What kind of building are they constructing? What is the purpose of the building?" In the same way, when people stop to consider their lives, they may become introspective and ask, "Is there some purpose to life?" Just as we assume that the unusual computer and the workers are there for a purpose, likewise people often assume that their lives must have some ultimate goal. In this chapter we will consider how various authors have discussed life's meaning.

Richard Robinson writes that life has no meaning. Since he believes that there is no god, there cannot be a particular goal or meaning for our lives. As a result, Robinson challenges his readers to create their own purpose for life.

In contrast to Robinson, Charles Colson explains how he discovered meaning for his life through his new relationship with God. Colson finds a sense of overwhelming relief and peace when he comes to see God as personal and real in his life.

Riane Eisler considers the question of meaning from a different perspective. Rather than considering one individual's search for meaning, Eisler finds meaning by looking at the broader history of humanity. She explains how societies in the past made mistakes and why humanity, as a whole, needs to find a new sense of direction and hope for the future.

Emil Brunner also looks into the past to find wisdom for the future. He explains that viewing God as our Creator gives life today a sense of meaning. Brunner challenges his readers to start at the beginning, at the original design God had for the universe. Given this starting point, humans can begin to discover the purpose of their collective and individual lives.

In contrast to those who focus on the past, Brooke Medicine Eagle writes that we should focus on the present. She writes that the "Great Spirit" of the universe is within each one of us. Instead of going beyond ourselves to find meaning, Medicine Eagle asks her readers to consider the divine resources which already exist within us. When discussing the meaning of life, some people say that each human creates his or her own meaning. Some writers believe that meaning comes from discovering inner resources which we normally overlook. Some people find meaning by discovering our place in the great movement of history. Some find meaning by discovering God.

"The finest achievement for humanity is to recognize our predicament, including our insecurity and our coming extinction, and to maintain our cheerfulness and love and decency in spite of it."

Life Has No Purpose—We Create It

Richard Robinson

Richard Robinson was educated at Oxford University in England. From 1928 to 1946 he taught philosophy at Cornell University in Ithaca, New York. In 1946 he returned to Oxford to teach. This viewpoint is from his book, *An Atheist's Values*. Robinson believes that the atheist's view of life requires greater strength and commitment than the theist's view of life. By denying the existence of God, Robinson feels that he has taken on more responsibilities in life, not less.

As you read, consider the following questions:
1. Robinson writes that people are insecure. Why are people insecure, and what importance does this have in their lives?
2. The author states that the atheist's approach to life is nobler than the theist's approach. Do you agree with his explanation? Explain.
3. According to Robinson, what values and attitudes should guide our lives?

Excerpted from *An Atheist's Values*, by Richard Robinson (Oxford: Blackwell, 1975). Reprinted by permission of the publisher.

The human situation is this. Each one of us dies. He ceases to pulse or breathe or move or think. He decays and loses his identity. His mind or soul or spirit ends with the ending of his body, because it is entirely dependent on his body.

The human species too will die one day, like all species of life. One day there will be no more men. This is not quite so probable as that each individual man will die; but it is over-whelmingly probable all the same. It seems very unlikely that we could keep the race going forever by hopping from planet to planet as each in turn cooled down. Only in times of extraordinary prosperity like the present could we ever travel to another planet at all.

We are permanently insecure. We are permanently in danger of loss, damage, misery, and death.

There Is No Secret to the Universe

Our insecurity is due partly to our ignorance. There is a vast amount that we do not know, and some of it is very relevant to our survival and happiness. It is not just one important thing that we can ascertain and live securely ever after. That one important thing would then deserve to be called 'the secret of the universe'. But there is no one secret of the universe. On the contrary, there are inexhaustibly many things about the universe that we need to know but do not know. There is no possibility of 'making sense of the universe', if that means discovering one truth about it which explains everything else about it and also explains itself. Our ignorance grows progressively less, at least during periods of enormous prosperity like the present time; but it cannot disappear, and must always leave us liable to unforeseen disasters.

The main cause of our insecurity is the limitedness of our power. What happens to us depends largely on forces we cannot always control. This will remain so throughout the life of our species, although our power will probably greatly increase.

There Is No God

There is no god to make up for the limitations of our power, to rescue us whenever the forces affecting us get beyond our control, or provide us hereafter with an incorruptible haven of absolute security. We have no superhuman father who is perfectly competent and benevolent as we perhaps once supposed our actual father to be.

What attitude ought we to take up, in view of this situation?

It would be senseless to be rebellious, since there is no god to rebel against. It would be wrong to let disappointment or terror or apathy or folly overcome us. It would be wrong to be sad or sarcastic or cynical or indignant. . . .

Cheerfulness is part of courage, and courage is an essential part of the right attitude. Let us not tell ourselves a comforting tale of a father in heaven because we are afraid to be alone, but bravely and cheerfully face whatever appears to be the truth.

Life's Purpose

It is frequently argued that religion gives men a purpose for living, namely, to please some god and win eternal bliss in heaven. And many men do need some great purpose for which to live. But it would be far more socially beneficial to induce men to accept the promotion of human welfare on earth as their major purpose in life. There is no evidence that any man has ever achieved bliss in heaven, but we can observe innumerable gains in human welfare in all countries. Moreover, men can achieve far greater and more immediate personal satisfaction from success in their efforts to promote human welfare in this world than from any effort to achieve bliss in the next world. And the observation of visible success is bound to strengthen any purpose.

Burnham P. Beckwith, *American Atheist*, March 1986.

The theist sometimes rebukes the pleasure-seeker by saying: *We were not put here to enjoy ourselves; man has a sterner and nobler purpose than that.* The atheist's conception of man is, however, still sterner and nobler than that of the theist. According to the theist we were put here by an all-powerful and all-benevolent god who will give us eternal victory and happiness if we only obey him. According to the atheist our situation is far sterner than that. There is no one to look after us but ourselves, and we shall certainly be defeated.

As our situation is far sterner than the theist dares to think, so our possible attitude towards it is far nobler than he conceives. When we contemplate the friendless position of man in the universe, as it is right sometimes to do, our attitude should be the tragic poet's affirmation of man's ideals of behaviour. Our dignity, and our finest occupation, is to assert and maintain our own self-chosen goods as long as we can, those great goods of beauty and truth and virtue. And among the virtues it is proper to mention in this connection above all the virtues of courage and love. There is no person in this universe to love us except ourselves; therefore let us love one another. The human race is alone; but individual men need not be alone, because we have each other. We are brothers without a father; let us all the more for that behave brotherly to each other. The finest achievement for humanity is to recognize our predicament, including our insecurity and our coming extinction, and to maintain our cheerfulness and love and decency in spite of it. We have good things to contemplate and high things to do. Let us do them.

Facing the Future with Hope

We ought to stand up and look the world frankly in the face. We ought to make the best we can of the world, and if it is not so good as we wish, after all it will still be better than what these others have made of it in all these ages. A good world needs knowledge, kindliness, and courage; it does not need a regretful hankering after the past or a fettering of the free intelligence by the words uttered long ago by ignorant men. It needs a fearless outlook and a free intelligence. It needs hope for the future, not looking back all the time toward a past that is dead, which we trust will be far surpassed by the future that our intelligence can create.

Betrand Russell, *Why I Am Not a Christian*, 1957.

We need to create and spread symbols and procedures that will confirm our intentions without involving us in intellectual dishonesty. This need is urgent today. For we have as yet no strong ceremonies to confirm our resolves except religious ceremonies, and most of us cannot join in religious ceremonies with a good conscience. When the *Titanic* went down, people sang 'nearer, my God, to thee'. When the Gloucesters were in prison in North Korea they strengthened themselves with religious ceremonies. At present we know no other way to strengthen ourselves in our most test-ing and tragic times. Yet this way has become dishonest. That is why it is urgent for us to create new ceremonies, through which to find strength without falsehood in these terrible sit-uations. It is not enough to formulate honest and high ideals. We must also create the ceremonies and the atmosphere that will hold them before us at all times. I have no conception how to do this; but I believe it will be done if we try.

> "*And then I prayed my first real prayer. 'God, I don't know how to find You, but I'm going to try! I'm not much the way I am now, but somehow I want to give myself to You.'*"

Finding Personal Peace with God Gives Life Purpose

Charles W. Colson

The following viewpoint is taken from *Born Again*, an autobiography by one of President Richard M. Nixon's top aides. In the book, Charles W. Colson tells how he and others labored to promote Nixon's reelection to the presidency in 1972 and about the Watergate Crisis which followed. During the crisis the public slowly learned about Nixon's abuses of power. Eventually Nixon had to resign from office. In the middle of this national crisis, Colson found himself in a very personal, spiritual crisis. In his book, *Born Again*, Colson gives an account of how he found God while talking to a friend, Tom Phillips, president of Raytheon (a high-tech research and manufacturing corporation). Later, Colson was sent to federal prison for his part in Watergate. After serving his time, Colson started an organization to spread Christianity in prisons.

As you read, consider the following questions:

1. Colson had known about Christianity before. What makes his conversation with Tom Phillips so special?
2. Colson says that he has "intellectual hang-ups to get past" before becoming a Christian. What role does the intellect have in Christianity?
3. What does the quote "pride is spiritual cancer" mean?

Excerpted from *Born Again*, by Charles W. Colson (Old Tappan, NJ: Chosen Books). Copyright © 1976 by Charles W. Colson. Reprinted by permission of Baker Book House Company.

"Tell me, Chuck," he began, "are you okay?" It was the same question he had asked in March.

As the President's confidant and so-called big-shot Washington lawyer I was still keeping my guard up. "I'm not doing too badly, I guess. All of this Watergate business, all the accusations—I suppose it's wearing me down some. But I'd rather talk about you, Tom. You've changed and I'd like to know what happened."

Tom drank from his glass and sat back reflectively. Briefly he reviewed his past, the rapid rise to power at Raytheon [Corporation]: executive vice-president at thirty-seven, president when he was only forty. He had done it with hard work, day and night, nonstop.

"The success came, all right, but something was missing," he mused. "I felt a terrible emptiness. Sometimes I would get up in the middle of the night and pace the floor of my bedroom or stare out into the darkness for hours at a time."

"I don't understand it," I interrupted. "I knew you in those days, Tom. You were a straight arrow, good family life, successful, everything in fact going your way."

"All that may be true, Chuck, but my life wasn't complete. I would go to the office each day and do my job, striving all the time to make the company succeed, but there was a big hole in my life. I began to read the Scriptures, looking for answers. Something made me realize I needed a personal relationship with God, forced me to search."

A prickly feeling ran down my spine. Maybe what I had gone through in the past several months wasn't so unusual after all—except I had not sought spiritual answers. I had not even been aware that finding a personal relationship with God was possible. I pressed him to explain the apparent contradiction between the emptiness inside while seeming to enjoy the affluent life.

"It may be hard to understand," Tom chuckled. "But I didn't seem to have anything that mattered. It was all on the surface. All the material things in life are meaningless if a man hasn't discovered what's underneath them.". . .

"One night I was in New York on business and noticed that Billy Graham was having a Crusade in Madison Square Garden," Tom continued. "I went—curious, I guess—hoping maybe I'd find some answers. What Graham said that night put it all into place for me. I saw what was missing, the personal relationship with Jesus Christ, the fact that I hadn't ever asked Him into my life, hadn't turned my life over to Him. So I did it—that very night at the Crusade."

Tom's tall, gangling frame leaned toward me, silhouetted by the yellow light behind him. Though his face was shaded, I could see his eyes begin to glisten and his voice became softer. "I asked Christ to come into my life and I could feel His presence with me, His peace within me. I could sense His Spirit there with me. Then I went out for a walk alone on the streets of New York. I never liked New York before, but this night it was beautiful. I walked for blocks and blocks, I guess. Everything seemed different to me. It was raining softly and the city lights created a golden glow. Something had happened to me and I knew it."

"That's what you mean by accepting Christ—you just ask?" I was more puzzled than ever.

"That's it, as simple as that," Tom replied. "Of course, you have to want Jesus in your life, really want Him. That's the way it starts. And let me tell you, things then begin to change. Since then I have found a satisfaction and a joy about living that I simply never knew was possible."

To me Jesus had always been an historical figure, but Tom explained that you could hardly invite Him into your life if you didn't believe that He is alive today and that His Spirit is a part of today's scene. I was moved by Tom's story even though I couldn't imagine how such a miraculous change could take place in such a simple way. Yet the excitement in Tom's voice as he described his experience was convincing and Tom was indeed different. More alive.

Watergate and the Soul

Then Tom turned the conversation again to my plight. I described some of the agonies of Watergate, the pressures I was under, how unfairly I thought the press was treating me. I was being defensive and when I ran out of explanations, Tom spoke gently but firmly.

"You know that I supported Nixon in this past election, but you guys made a serious mistake. You would have won the election without any of the hanky-panky. Watergate and the dirty tricks were so unnecessary. And it was wrong, just plain wrong. You didn't have to do it."

Tom was leaning forward, elbows on his knees, his hands stretched forward almost as if he was trying to reach out for me. There was an urgent appeal in his eyes. "Don't you understand that?" he asked with such genuine feeling that I couldn't take offense.

"If only you had believed in the rightness of your cause, none of this would have been necessary. None of this would have happened. The problem with all of you, including you, Chuck—you simply had to go for the other guy's jugular. You had to try to destroy your enemies. You had to destroy them because you couldn't trust in yourselves."

The heat at that moment seemed unbearable as I wiped away drops of perspiration over my lip. The iced tea was soothing as I sipped it, although with Tom's points hitting home so painfully, I longed for a Scotch and soda. To myself I admitted that Tom was on target: the world of *us* against *them* as we saw it from our insulated White House enclave—the Nixon White House against the world. Insecure about our cause, our overkill approach was a way to play it safe. And yet . . . .

"Tom, one thing you don't understand. In politics it's dog-eat-dog; you simply can't survive otherwise. I've been in the political business for twenty years, including several campaigns right here in Massachusetts. I know how things are done. Politics is like war. If you don't keep the enemy on the defensive, you'll be on the defensive yourself. Tom, this man Nixon has been under constant attack all of his life. The only way he could make it was to fight back. Look at the criticism he took over Vietnam. Yet he was right. We never would have made it if we hadn't fought the way we did, hitting our critics, never letting them get the best of us. We didn't have any choice."

Even as I talked, the words sounded more and more empty to me. Tired old lines, I realized. I was describing the ways of the political world, all right, while suddenly wondering if there could be a better way.

Tom believed so, anyway. He was so gentle I couldn't re-sent what he said as he cut right through it all: "Chuck, I hate to say this, but you guys brought it on yourselves. If you had put your faith in God, and if your cause were just, He would have guided you. And His help would have been a thousand times more powerful than all your phony ads and shady schemes put together."

With any other man the notion of relying on God would have seemed to me pure Pollyanna. Yet I had to be impressed with the way this man ran his company in the equally competitive world of business: ignoring his enemies, trying to follow God's ways. Since his conversion Raytheon had never done better, sales and profits soaring. Maybe there was something to it; anyway it's tough to argue with success.

"Chuck, I don't think you will understand what I'm saying about God until you are willing to face yourself honestly and squarely. This is the first step." Tom reached to the corner table and picked up a small paperback book. I read the title: *Mere Christianity* by C.S. Lewis.

"I suggest you take this with you and read it while you are on vacation." Tom started to hand it to me, then paused. "Let me read you one chapter." . . .

The Cancer of Pride

As he read, I could feel a flush coming into my face and a curious burning sensation that made the night seem even warmer. Lewis's words seemed to pound straight at me. . . .

Suddenly I felt naked and unclean, my bravado defenses gone. I was exposed, unprotected, for Lewis's words were describing me. As he continued, one passage in particular seemed to sum up what had happened to all of us at the White House:

> For Pride is spiritual cancer: it eats up the very possibility of love, or contentment, or even common sense.

Just as a man about to die is supposed to see flash before him, sequence by sequence, the high points of his life, so, as Tom's voice read on that August evening, key events in my life paraded before me as if projected on a screen. Things I hadn't thought about in years—my graduation speech at prep school—being "good enough" for the Marines—my first marriage, into the "right" family—sitting on the Jaycees' dais while civic leader after civic leader praised me as the outstanding young man of Boston—then to the White House—the clawing and straining for status and position—"Mr. Colson, the President is calling—Mr. Colson, the President wants to see you right away." . . .

Now, sitting there on the dimly lit porch, my self-centered past was washing over me in waves. It was painful. Agony. Desperately I tried to defend myself. What about my sacrifices for government service, the giving up of a big income, putting my stocks into a blind trust? The truth, I saw in an instant, was that I'd wanted the position in the White House more than I'd wanted money. There was no sacrifice. And the more I had talked about my own sacrifices, the more I was really trying to build myself up in the eyes of others. I would eagerly have given up everything I'd ever earned to prove myself at the mountaintop of government. It was pride—Lewis's "great sin"—that had propelled me through life.

Tom finished the chapter on pride and shut the book. I mumbled something noncommittal to the effect that "I'll look forward to reading that." But Lewis's torpedo had hit me amidships. I think Phillips knew it as he stared into my eyes. That one chapter ripped through the protective armor in which I had unknowingly encased myself for forty-two years. Of course, I had not known God. *How could I?* I had been concerned with myself. *I* had done this and that, *I* had achieved, *I* had succeeded and *I* had given God none of the credit, never once thanking Him for any of His gifts to me. I had never thought of anything being "immeasurably superior" to myself, or if I had in fleeting moments thought about the infinite power of God, I had not related Him to my life. In those brief moments while Tom read, I saw myself as I never had before. And the picture was ugly,

"How about it, Chuck?" Tom's question jarred me out of my trance. I knew precisely what he meant. Was I ready to make the leap of faith as he had in New York, to "accept" Christ?

Hesitations to Faith

"Tom, you've shaken me up. I'll admit that. That chapter describes me. But I can't tell you I'm ready to make the kind of commitment you did. I've got to be certain. I've got to learn a lot more, be sure all my reservations are satisfied. I've got a lot of intellectual hang-ups to get past."

For a moment Tom looked disappointed, then he smiled. "I understand, I understand."

Touched by God

I was eight years old. We were in California en route to Hawaii, where my parents were assuming a new pastorate.

"Oil Town, U.S.A." [a movie produced by the Billy Graham Evangelistic Association] was being shown in Santa Rosa. My twin sister, Jan, and I went. It was a wonderful movie. A movie of love and obedience and the pull of the world.

Even as a small girl I understood that to say "yes" to Jesus sometimes meant hurt and sacrifice.

It always involves courage.

At the close of the film, in a big auditorium, a man asked if anyone would like to invite Jesus Christ into his life. I had known about Jesus all my eight years, but I never felt conviction, and I had never chosen to let him into my life.

That night I started to cry.

I cried not because someone tapped me on the shoulder or because my dad was sitting next to me or because the movie made me sad.

I cried because God touched me.

I knew I was a sinner, and I knew I wanted him.

That night, in a simple cotton dress and with her hair pulled back into a ponytail, a little girl en route to Honolulu, Hawaii, with her parents found Jesus Christ.

And I have never been the same.

Ann Kiemel, in *Wondrous Power, Wondrous Love*, 1983.

"You see," I continued, "I saw men turn to God in the Marine Corps; I did once myself. Then afterwards it's all forgotten and everything is back to normal. Foxhole religion is just a way of using God. How can I make a commitment now? My whole world is crashing down around me. How can I be sure I'm not just running for shelter and that when the crisis is over I'll forget it? I've got to answer all the intellectual arguments first and if I can do that, I'll be sure."

"I understand," Tom repeated quietly.

I was relieved he did, yet deep inside of me something wanted to tell Tom to press on. He was making so much sense, the first time anyone ever had in talking about God.

But Tom did not press on. He handed me his copy of *Mere Christianity*. "Once you've read this, you might want to read the Book of John in the Bible." I scribbled notes of the key passages he quoted. "Also there's a man in Washington you should meet," he continued, "name of Doug Coe. He gets people together for Christian fellowship—prayer breakfasts and things like that. I'll ask him to contact you."

Tom then reached for his Bible and read a few of his favorite psalms. The comforting words were like a cold soothing ointment. For the first time in my life, familiar verses I'd heard chanted lifelessly in church came alive. "Trust in the Lord," I remember Tom reading, and I wanted to, right that moment I wanted to—if only I knew how, if only I could be sure.

"Would you like to pray together, Chuck?" Tom asked, closing his Bible and putting it on the table beside him.

Startled, I emerged from my deep thoughts. "Sure—I guess I would—Fine." I'd never prayed with anyone before except when someone said grace before a meal. Tom bowed his head, folded his hands, and leaned forward on the edge of his seat. "Lord," he began, "we pray for Chuck and his family, that You might open his heart and show him the light and the way. . . ."

As Tom prayed, something began to flow into me—a kind of energy. Then came a wave of emotion which nearly brought tears. I fought them back. It sounded as if Tom were speaking directly and personally to God, almost as if He were sitting beside us. The only prayers I'd ever heard were formal and stereotyped, sprinkled with *Thees* and *Thous*.

When he finished, there was a long silence. I knew he expected me to pray but I didn't know what to say and was too self-conscious to try. We walked to the kitchen together where Gert [Tom Phillips' wife] was still at the big table, reading. I thanked her and Tom for their hospitality.

"Come back, won't you?" she said. Her smile convinced me she meant it.

"Take care of yourself, Chuck, and let me know what you think of that book, will you?" With that, Tom put his hand on my shoulder and grinned. "I'll see you soon."

I didn't say much; I was afraid my voice would crack, but I had the strong feeling that I *would* see him soon. And I couldn't wait to read his little book.

Turning to God

Outside in the darkness, the iron grip I'd kept on my emotions began to relax. Tears welled up in my eyes as I groped in the darkness for the right key to start my car. Angrily I brushed them away and started the engine. "What kind of weakness is this?" I said to nobody.

The tears spilled over and suddenly I knew I had to go back into the house and pray with Tom. I turned off the motor, got out of the car. As I did, the kitchen light went out, then the light in the dining room. Through the hall window I saw Tom stand aside as Gert started up the stairs ahead of him. Now the hall was in darkness. It was too late. I stood for a moment staring at the darkened house, only one light burning now in an upstairs bedroom. Why hadn't I prayed when he gave me the chance? I wanted to so badly. Now I was alone, really alone.

As I drove out of Tom's driveway, the tears were flowing uncontrollably. There were no streetlights, no moonlight. The car headlights were flooding illumination before my eyes, but I was crying so hard it was like trying to swim underwater. I pulled to the side of the road not more than a hundred yards from the entrance to Tom's driveway, the tires sinking into soft mounds of pine needles.

I remember hoping that Tom and Gert wouldn't hear my sobbing, the only sound other than the chirping of crickets that penetrated the still of the night. With my face cupped in my hands, head leaning forward against the wheel, I forgot about machismo, about pretenses, about fears of being weak. And as I did, I began to experience a wonderful feeling of being released. Then came the strange sensation that water was not only running down my cheeks, but surging through my whole body as well, cleansing and cooling as it went. They weren't tears of sadness and remorse, nor of joy—but somehow, tears of relief.

And then I prayed my first real prayer. "God, I don't know how to find You, but I'm going to try! I'm not much the way I am now, but somehow I want to give myself to You." I didn't know how to say more, so I repeated over and over the words: *Take me*.

> *"Let us reaffirm our ancient covenant, our sacred bond with our Mother, the Goddess of nature and spirituality."*

Ecofeminism Gives Life Purpose

Riane Eisler

Riane Eisler is the author of the international bestseller *The Chalice and the Blade* and the co-founder of the Center for Partnership Studies, a research and educational center in Pacific Grove, California. In her book, Eisler reinterprets ancient history and modern archaeological findings to support ecofeminism, a philosophy in which people live in sexual and social equality in harmony with nature. She calls this lifestyle "a partnership way." In the following viewpoint, Eisler issues a manifesto, rejecting what she calls the current patriarchal and male-dominated society that now exists and calling for a return to the ecofeminist traditions of the past.

As you read, consider the following questions:
1. What is the Gaia hypothesis, according to Eisler?
2. How does the author distinguish between dominator and partnership societies?
3. What kind of future for humankind does Eisler envision?

Excerpted from Riane Eisler, "The Gaia Tradition and the Partnership Future: An Ecofeminist Manifesto," in *Reweaving the World*, edited by Irene Diamond and Gloria F. Orenstein (San Francisco: Sierra Club Books, 1990). Reprinted by permission of the publisher.

The leading-edge social movements of our time—the peace, feminist, and ecology movements, and ecofeminism, which integrates all three—are in some respects very new. But they also draw from very ancient traditions only now being reclaimed due to what British archaeologist James Mellaart calls a veritable revolution in archaeology.

These traditions go back thousands of years. Scientific archaeological methods are now making it possible to document the way people lived and thought in prehistoric times. One fascinating discovery about our past is that for millennia—a span of time many times longer than the 5,000 years conventionally counted as history—prehistoric societies worshipped the Goddess of nature and spirituality, our great Mother, the giver of life and creator of all. But even more fascinating is that these ancient societies were structured very much like the more peaceful and just society we are now trying to construct.

A Reverence for the Earth

This is not to say that these were ideal societies or utopias. But, unlike our societies, they were *not* warlike. They were *not* societies where women were subordinate to men. And they did *not* see our Earth as an object for exploitation and domination.

In short, they were societies that had what we today call an ecological consciousness: the awareness that the Earth must be treated with reverence and respect. And this reverence for the life-giving and life-sustained powers of the Earth was rooted in a social structure where women and "feminine" values such as caring, compassion, and non-violence were not subordinate to men and the so-called masculine values of conquest and domination. Rather, the life-giving powers incarnated in women's bodies were given the highest social value. . . .

The Gaia Tradition

We now know that there was not one cradle of civilization in Sumer about 3,500 years ago. Rather, there were many cradles of civilization, all of them thousands of years older. And thanks to far more scientific and extensive archaeological excavations, we also know that in these highly creative societies women held important social positions as priestesses, craftspeople, and elders of matrilineal clans. Contrary to what we have been taught of the Neolithic or first agrarian civilizations as male dominated and highly violent, these were generally peaceful societies in which both women and men lived in harmony with one another and nature. Moreover, in all these peaceful cradles of civilization, to borrow Merlin Stone's arresting phrase from the book of the same title, "God was a woman" (New York: Dial Press, 1976).

The Goddess Rather than God

I used to think of the divine as "God." Now, if I think in terms of a personalized deity at all, I think more of the Goddess than of the God. I feel very strongly that our society's denial of the feminine aspect of the deity, the Mother aspect, is one of the great obstacles to having that personal relationship, that direct connection with the divine.

Riane Eisler in *For the Love of God*, 1990.

There is today much talk about the Gaia hypothesis (so called because Gaia is the Greek name for the Earth). This is a new scientific theory proposed by biologists Lynn Margulis and James Lovelock that our planet is a living system designed to maintain and to nurture life. But what is most striking about the Gaia hypothesis is that in essence it is a scientific update of the belief system of Goddess-worshipping prehistoric societies. In these societies the world was viewed as the great Mother, a living entity who in both her temporal and spiritual manifestations creates and nurtures all forms of life. . . .

Dominator and Partnership Societies

Even in the nineteenth century, when archaeology was still in its infancy, scholars found evidence of societies where women were not subordinate to men. But their interpretation of this evidence was that if these societies were not patriarchies, they must have been matriarchies. In other words, if men did not dominate women, then women must have dominated men. However, this conclusion is not borne out by the evidence. Rather, it is a function of what I have called a *dominator* society worldview. The real alternative to patriarchy is not matriarchy, which is only the other side of the dominator coin. The alternative, now revealed to be the original direction of our cultural evolution, is what I call a *partnership* society: a way of organizing human relations in which beginning with the most fundamental difference in our species—the difference between female and male—diversity is *not* equated with inferiority or superiority.

What we have until now been taught as history is only the history of dominator species—the record of the male dominant, authoritarian, and highly violent civilizations that began about 5,000 years ago. For example, the conventional view is that the beginning of European civilization is marked by the emergence in ancient Greece of the Indo-Europeans. But the new archaeological evidence demonstrates that the arrival of the Indo-Europeans actually marks the truncation of European civilization. That is, as Marija Gimbutas extensively documents, there was in Greece and the Balkans an earlier civilization, which she calls the civilization of Old Europe (*The Goddesses and Gods of Old Europe*, 1982). The first Indo-European invasions (by pastoralists from the arid steppes of the northeast) foreshadow the end of a matrifocal, matrilineal, peaceful agrarian era. Like fingerprints in the archaeological record, we see evidence of how wave after wave of barbarian invaders from the barren fringes of the globe leave in their wake destruction and what archaeologists call cultural impoverishment. And what characterizes these invaders is that they bring with them male dominance along with their angry gods of thunder and war. . . .

The Goddess Was the Source of All Life

We have been taught that in "Western tradition," religion is the spiritual realm and that spirituality is separate from, and superior to, nature. But for our Goddess-worshipping ancestors, spirituality and nature were one. In the religion of Western partnership societies, there was no need for the artificial distinction between spirituality and nature or for the exclusion of half of humanity from spiritual power.

In sharp contrast to "traditional" patriarchal religions (where only men can be priests, rabbis, bishops, lamas, Zen masters, and popes), we know from Minoan, Egyptian,

Sumerian, and other ancient records that women were once priestesses. Indeed, the highest religious office appears to have been that of high priestess in service of the Goddess. And the Goddess herself was not only the source of all life and nature; she was also the font of spirituality, mercy, wisdom, and justice. For example, as the Sumerian Goddess Nanshe, she sought justice for the poor and shelter for the weak. The Egyptian Goddess Maat was also the goddess of justice. The Greek Goddess Demeter was known as the lawgiver, the bringer of civilization, dispensing mercy and justice. As the Celtic Goddess Cerridwen, she was the goddess of intelligence and knowledge. And it is Gaia, the primeval prophetess of the shrine of Delphi, who in Greek mythology is said to have given the golden apple tree (the tree of knowledge) to her daughter, the Goddess Hera. Moreover, the Greek Fates, the enforcers of laws, are female. And so also are the Greek Muses, who inspire all creative endeavor. . . .

We Must Reclaim the Great Mother

I believe that the denial of our connection with the Mother aspect, the feminine aspect of the deity, is one of the major obstacles to achieving that meaningful and fulfilling personal relationship not only with the deity but with one another. We all can observe the element of the feminine, of the Mother, of the nurturer, from our experiences of a mother. The Great Mother also has a dark aspect, however: the transformative aspect of reclaiming life at death. But to have been deprived of that motherly dimension in the deity reflects something in our dominator society: a deadening of empathy, a deadening of caring, a denial of the feminine in men, and a contempt for women and the feminine.

Riane Eisler in *For the Love of God*, 1990.

We also know from a number of contemporary tribal societies that the separation between nature and spirituality is not universal. Tribal peoples generally think of nature in spiritual terms. Nature spirits must be respected, indeed, revered. And we also know that in many of these tribal societies women as well as men can be shamans or spiritual healers and that descent in these tribes is frequently traced through the mother.

In sum, *both* nature and woman can partake of spirituality in societies oriented to a partnership model. In such societies there is no need for a false dichotomy between a "masculine" spirituality and "feminine" nature. Moreover, since in ancient partnership societies woman and the Goddess were identified with *both* nature and spirituality, neither woman nor nature were devalued and exploited. . . .

We Must Rediscover the Goddess of Spirituality

For many thousands of years, millennia longer than the 5,000 years we count as recorded history, everything was done in a sacred manner. Planting and harvesting fields were rites of spring and autumn celebrated in a ritual way. Baking bread from grains, molding pots out of clay, weaving cloth out of fibers, carving tools out of metals—all these ways of technologically melding culture and nature were sacred ceremonies. There was then no splintering of culture and nature, spirituality, science, and technology. Both our intuition and our reason were applied to the building of civilization, to devising better ways for us to live and work cooperatively.

The rediscovery of these traditions signals a way out of our alienation from one another and from nature. In our time, when the nuclear bomb and advanced technology threaten all life on this planet, the reclamation of these traditions can be the basis for the restructuring of society: the completion of the modern transformation from a dominator to a partnership world.

Poised on the brink of ecocatastrophe, let us gain the courage to look at the world anew, to reverse custom, to transcend our limitations, to break free from the conventional constraints, the conventional views of what are knowledge and truth. Let us understand that we cannot graft peace and ecological balance on a dominator system; that a just and egalitarian society is impossible without the full and equal partnership of women and men.

Let us reaffirm our ancient covenant, our sacred bond with our Mother, the Goddess of nature and spirituality. Let us renounce the worship of angry gods wielding thunderbolts or swords. Let us once again honor the chalice, the ancient symbol of the power to create and enhance life—and let us understand that this power is not woman's alone but also man's.

A Renewed Understanding

For ourselves, and for the sake of our children and their children, let us use our human thrust for creation rather than destruction. Let us teach our sons and daughters that men's conquest of nature, of women, and of other men is not a heroic virtue; that we have the knowledge and the capacity to survive; that we need not blindly follow our bloodstained path to planetary death; that we can reawaken from our 5,000-year dominator nightmare and allow our evolution to resume its interrupted course.

While there is still time, let us fulfill our promise. Let us reclaim the trees of knowledge and of life. Let us regain our lost sense of wonder and reverence for the miracles of life and love, let us learn again to live in partnership so we may fulfill our responsibility to ourselves and to our Great Mother, this wondrous planet Earth.

"There is One who knows the destiny of the world, He, who first made the sketch, He who created and rules the world according to this plan."

God's Creation of Everything Gives Life Purpose

Emil Brunner

Emil Brunner (1889–1966), a theologian from Switzerland, wrote many books on theology and Christian living during his life. In this viewpoint, Brunner argues the importance of recognizing that God is the Creator of everything. Once a person accepts the fact that God is the source of everything, that person's life and thoughts can begin to have meaning and harmony.

As you read, consider the following questions:

1. Why does Brunner compare God to a king and to an artist?
2. Why does the author write: "Chance? What harebrained superstition!"?
3. How does a person come to understand God's plans and reasons?

Reprinted from *Our Faith*, by Emil Brunner (New York: Scribner's, 1936).

For just as in a royal palace everything is royally administered, or as in a great artist's house the whole house testifies of the artist, even if he is not seen, so, too, the world is the house of the Great King and the Great Artist. He does not permit himself to be seen; for man cannot see God, only the world. But this world is His creation, and whether conscious of it or not, it speaks of Him who made it. Yet in spite of this testimony man does not know Him, or at least not rightly.

We Are Surrounded by Miracles

Every man has two hands each of which is a greater work of art than anything else that human ingenuity has created; but men are so obsessed with their own doings that they acclaim every human creation and make a great display over it, yet fail to discern God's miraculous deeds. Every one has two eyes. Have you ever thought of how astounding a miracle is a seeing eye, the window of the soul? Yes, even more than a window; one might even call the eye the soul itself gazing and visible. Who has so made it that the hundred millions of rod and cone cells which together make sight possible, are so co-ordinated that they can give sight? Chance? What harebrained superstition! Truly, you do not behold man alone through the eye, but the Creator as well. Yet we fools do not perceive Him. We behave ourselves in this God-created world (if one may use the clumsy simile) like dogs in a great art gallery. We see the pictures and yet fail to see them, for if we saw them rightly we would see the Creator too. Our madness, haughtiness, irreverence—in short, our sin, is the reason for our failure to see the Creator in His creation.

And yet He speaks so loudly that we cannot fail to hear His voice. For this reason the peoples of all ages, even when they have not known the Creator, have had some presentiments of Him. There is no religion in which there is not some sort of surmise of the Creator. But men have never known Him rightly. The book of Nature does not suffice to reveal the Creator aright to such unintelligent and obdurate pupils as ourselves.

The Creator has therefore given us another, even more clearly written book in which to know Him—the Bible. In it

He has also drawn His own portrait so that we must all perceive that He is truly the Creator. The name of this picture is Jesus Christ. In him we know the Creator for the first as He really is. For in him we know God's purpose for His creation.

God first revealed Himself to the children of Israel as the Creator. At that time the world was replete with religions, but they did not honor the one Lord of all the world. The gods of the heathen are partly constructions of human fantasy, partly surmise of the true God, a wild combination of both. The great thinkers like Plato and Aristotle spoke indeed of a divinity that pervaded all things. But they did not know the living God. It pleased God to reveal Himself to the little people of Israel as the Lord God. That means—the God whom we may not use as one uses a porter—as the heathen use their gods. And as the God whom one cannot conceive as the philosophers think of Him, an "idea of God." But to Israel He was revealed as one who encounters man and claims Him as Lord. "I am the Lord thy God." "I will be your God and ye shall be my people." The Lord is He, to whom one belongs wholly, body and soul. The Lord is He who has an absolute claim to us, because we, and all that in us is, come from Him. The Lord God is also the Creator God, and only when we know Him as the Lord God do we know Him rightly as the Creator. The heathen, even their greatest thinkers, do not rightly know the difference between God and world, between God and man, between God and nature. These are all confused with one another. God first revealed Himself to Israel as the One who is over all the world, as its *Lord*, of whom, through whom and to whom it is created. That a divine being created the world—is not faith in the Creator, but a theory of the origin of the world, which signifies nothing. That God is the Creator means: *thy* Creator is the Lord of the world, *thy* Lord, you belong to Him totally. Without Him you are nothing, and in His hand is your life. He wants you for Himself: I am the Lord thy God, thou shalt have no other Gods (idols) before Me. That is as much to say: thou shalt love the Lord thy God with all thy heart and with all thy soul and with all thy strength. That is no lovely, interesting theory about the origin of the world; if you believe this, you are a "slave of God," your life then has another meaning, then you are really another man. Rather, you are now for the first time a man. To believe in God the Creator means to obey God the Lord.

Finding God's Plan in the Confusion

Looking down at night from the mountain top upon Zurich, the traveller sees a broad luminous strip in the midst of the confusing welter of the twinkling lights of the city. It is lovely and attractive although one does not understand the significance of this aggregation of lights. It is the park square in front of the railway station; each one of the hundreds of lights is in its place, but the wayfarer on the heights above knows nothing of this perfect order. Only the chief electrician knows why this arrangement has been made and not some other. He has the blue-print and can grasp the whole plan at a glance; it is his insight, his will that orders and guides the whole.

Just so, too, we may think of what takes place in the whole world. We poor insignificant humans are set down in the midst of the whole wild world and cannot survey it all. Here and there it may be, we can catch a glimpse of the wonderful order in nature, the regularity of the stars, scattered over the wide spaces of the universe yet obedient to one law; the order to be found even in the microscopic world, as also within visible things concerning which science has given such amazing information in recent years; the order in the construction of a flower or of an animal, from the flea to the whale, a noteworthy obedience to law even in the life of man. When, however, we ask, what does all this mean, what is its purpose, we know nothing definite.

We can advance clever theories and make guesses, and men have been doing so for ages and have expressed most curious opinions about the purpose of the happenings in the world: Each one has made his guess from the center of his tiny circle of experience. But who would want to build upon such a foundation? Who would dare say; yes, it is thus and so? Every one realizes that these are only humble opinions concerning something too sublime for our conception. We know neither where we nor the world are heading. In spite of all experiment and experience it remains for us a profound, impenetrable mystery. And that weighs heavily upon us. It is as though we were feeling our way in the dark. Whither? Why? What is the meaning of everything? What is the goal? Because we do not know that, we are apprehensive, despondent, troubled, like a man condemned to hard labor without knowing the reason why. Because we have no insight into the plan of the world we are dull and apathetic.

Defining Faith

Now faith is being sure of what we hope for and certain of what we do not see. This is what the ancients were commended for.

By faith we understand that the universe was formed at God's command, so that what is seen was not made out of what was visible.

The Bible, Hebrews 11:1–3.

There is One who knows the destiny of the world, He, who first made the sketch, He who created and rules the world according to this plan. What is confusion for us is order for Him, what we call chance is designed by Him, thought out from eternity and executed with omnipotence. It is indeed much to know "He thrones in might and doeth all things well." Chance? With this sorry word we merely admit that we do not know why things happen as they do. But God knows; God wills it. There is no chance, no more than any light in the station below just happens to be where it is. The chief Designer knows why, while we say, "chance," "fate." It is important to know that.

Indeed, in His great goodness, God has done even more. He did not want to leave us in the dark, for it is not His will that we should go plodding through life fearful, troubled, and apathetic, but that we, mere men though we are, should know something of His great world plans. He has, therefore, revealed to us the counsels of His will in His Word. He has not done it all at once—men would not have understood it at all. But, long ago, like a wise teacher He laid his plans. To Abraham, Moses, and the prophets He revealed more and more of His plans, making them ever clearer, until at last, "when the time was accomplished" He revealed His heart and let men behold what He had in mind, His goal. Then He brought forth His plan out of the darkness of mystery and revealed it to all the world: Jesus Christ, the Word of God in person, God's revelation of the meaning of universal history so that we need no longer walk in darkness but in the light. How different God's plans are than the ruminations of man upon the riddle of the world!

> *"Spirit is not something far off that you*
> *need to seek or . . . go to Tibet to find.*
> *Spirit lives in you, . . . in every cell."*

The Great Spirit Within Us Gives Life Purpose

Brooke Medicine Eagle

Brooke Medicine Eagle is a member of the Crow Indian tribe and is a grandniece of the famous Chief Joseph of the Nez Percé. She was given the name "Medicine Eagle" because she could "fly high and see far" as a visionary. She is a licensed counselor who conducts training camps, retreats, and ceremonies to help people find the spirit within themselves. In this viewpoint, Medicine Eagle challenges people to discover their relationship to the Great Spirit, the "All That Is."

As you read, consider the following questions:
1. When Medicine Eagle writes that people need to expand their attention, what does she mean?
2. Medicine Eagle emphasizes finding the unity or wholeness in our lives. How does her message compare to other religious beliefs?
3. Medicine Eagle explains that we need "healing." What does she mean?

From "Open to the Great Mystery," by Brooke Medicine Eagle, in *For the Love of God*, edited by Richard Carlson and Benjamin Shield; © 1990. Reprinted by permission of New World Library, Novato, CA 94949, www.newworldlibrary.com.

My relationship with God developed at an early age. I was raised on a remote little ranch, where I had for company and for the fullness of my life three other humans and an enormous amount of animals and land and sky and wind. As a child, my experience of God included everything—a love of the whole beauty around me. And the country was so beautiful: mountains that ended in aspen groves and streams, thick with wild animals and game of all kinds. One time I said to my mother, "You know, I think heaven is just like this, only the animals would speak to us, they wouldn't be afraid of us."

In developing a personal relationship with the Great Spirit, you first pay attention to the fact that you already have a relationship with Spirit. Spirit is not something far off that you need to seek or call or grab or go to Tibet to find. Spirit lives in you; it lives within your body, in every cell. You can touch the Great Spirit by touching into your own aliveness. All you need is a different attitude about how big you are, how deep you are, how high you are. You must be willing to own that you are God; even though you are a minute part of the All That Is, you are connected and one with it.

You Must Expand Your Attention Span

It is also good for you to develop another kind of attention and ability: to hold more and more of life, more and more of the holiness, the whole circle. An elder once asked me, "How long has it been since we sang in celebration of the life of the great whale? How long has it been since we danced in celebration of the life of the flowers? How long has it been since we danced in celebration of each and every part of life?" It's been much too long.

When we are newborns, we have attention only for our mothers. Our little faces look into their faces and that's all we see. Then perhaps father gets connected in; then the other siblings. Our ability to love or pay attention to or be connected with things begins to expand. We may belong to a clan or a group, and we can expand our arms and hold all its members inside our circle. Sometimes we become big enough to hold more, perhaps big enough to be called a Mother of the City. This person loves all the people, the whole city; loves and holds them in a good way and does good things in honor of them. Some people are Mothers of Nations. As we expand our attention we have the kind of love that can hold something that big. Mother Earth is enormous compared to that kind of love. She is big enough and loving enough to hold all of us in her arms all the time. When we expand our attention to the Great Mystery, to the All That Is—which is in and attentive to everything, because every cell, every tiny bit of matter, has consciousness in it—then we have an omniscient, omnipresent, powerful experience. We must build the ability to do that. When we talk about moving toward God realization, that's where we're moving.

Related to Nature

When I speak about attention, I mean literally, "How much attention can we pay to ourselves?" As children, sometimes we cannot hold our attention for more than a couple of seconds. Over the years we are able to attend to more and more. Yet, we're seldom schooled to hold life in respect, to enlarge our ability to love, take care of, and be respectfully connected with all things around us. In the old days, the primary job of the native Lakota mother was to teach the new child that he or she was connected with every thing in the circle of life. She would take the child walking and say, "See the squirrel? That's your brother. See the tree? We are related. This is your family; these are all your family." Because they were all brought up that way, they knew deeply that they were all interconnected, they were all family, they were all conscious. Lakota children had an opportunity to begin early in life to attend to the whole or the holiness, the spiritual side of things, and then to expand this ability powerfully as they grew.

We, too, can acknowledge that Spirit lives within us, that we are a part of God. The more we can love ourselves and attend to all of life around us with a loving, open, connected heart and good relationship, the more we can be in a very beautiful place. All it takes is practice.

Dialogue also is important in relating to the Great Spirit. It's not just my talking to the enormous All That Is. The All

71

That Is also talks to me—gives me information, support, nurturance, food. It's a totally open connection. In the Sacred Pipe of our Lakota people, the bowl represents the earth and all of life. The open wooden stem represents our eternal connection to the Great Spirit. The pipe has an open channel that our breath or vibration or energy or thought can go through. Not only can it go out, but it can also come in. When we breathe through the pipe, it's like drawing Spirit into us. We can draw in information, and we can send out whatever we want across the bridge to everything else by blowing out the smoke or by praying with just our breath, energy, thoughts, and gratitude.

The Earth Is Alive

When you understand the universe as a living being, then the split between religion and science disappears because religion no longer becomes a set of dogmas and beliefs we have to accept even though they don't make any sense, and science is no longer restricted to a type of analysis that picks the world apart. Science becomes our way of looking more deeply into this living being that we're all in, understanding it more deeply and clearly. This itself has a poetic dimension. I want to explore what it means when we really accept that this Earth is alive and that we are part of her being.

Starhawk, in *Reweaving the World*, 1990.

The channel is open in everyone. No one, whether priest or medicine man, needs to intercede or interpret or make that bridge any better, more open, more clear, more truthful, more sacred, or more holy. We have an open channel to the deepest, most beautiful part of ourselves, which is the same as our connection with everything. You don't need someone to put a hand on your head and say, "Yes, you're okay, and now you can talk to God." This priestly attitude assumes that you are not already in touch with Spirit and capable in that realm, although perhaps you may not be so practiced as some. That bridge to Spirit is always there, always open. You never need to stand at a toll gate on that bridge.

It's wonderful to be in the energy of elders and others who are practiced in that relationship with God. When that connection is humming, it's like a song going on. The elders give you suggestions and pray with you and hold you in their energy and light and wisdom as you go upon the mountain and have your own unique and powerful connection with Spirit.

It is very hard on people to assume that they don't have the ability to make that spiritual contact directly. It is sad that in the wider culture—and even now in native cultures, because of the breakup of old ways—there are very few who have the breadth and depth of attention to be holy people. Think how powerful it would be if our mothers really acknowledged, and were grateful for, our connection to everything. We would have turned out very differently.

The Hologram Example

Hologram theory offers a powerful example about who we are and who God is. A holographic picture is three dimensional. If you tear the picture in half, each half retains the same image and is still three dimensional. If you tear one of those halves in half, you still have the same dimensional image. No matter how many times you tear the fragments in half, the same image is still there. The tinier you tear it and the more times you tear it the dimmer it gets, the less distinct and real it becomes to your eyes.

I am and you are and we all are individual tiny pieces—all individuated or torn up out of the sheet that is God, that is All That Is. The whole picture is connected in us. It's all here. My little scrap may be torn to look a little different, but the whole picture is, in fact, within me. The exciting thing is that I can make that picture more distinct by joining my piece with your piece, and then with my family's piece, and then with my friend's piece, and on and on. The more I can attend to or connect myself with everything else around me, the more distinct the pictures become for us all. And we can reach out to others in the same way. Together we can acknowledge and enlarge our attentions so that we stand in a holy place—in a place that takes in the whole circle, a place that is healed in this wholeness, this holiness, a world that is healed and complete.

CHAPTER 3

How Do Religions Give Life Meaning?

Chapter Preface

Throughout history humans have held a wide array of religious beliefs. Some people have believed in a single God; others have believed in a pantheon of divine beings. Some believe in a personal God who responds to their prayers, while others view God as an impersonal force behind their world of daily experiences. For some people, God speaks clearly through prophets and written revelation. For others, God is discovered in their private meditations and in their willingness to open their minds or souls. Regardless of the particular belief system, religions very often dominate people's search for meaning in their lives.

Judaism, the religion of the Jews (or the Israelites), is based upon a self-revealing God. The most important revelation was the Law, which was given to Moses at Mount Sinai. In this chapter, Louis Finkelstein gives a brief explanation of Judaism. Finkelstein explains the role of the Law in Jewish life, various Jewish traditions, and three sub-divisions in Judaism today. He concludes with a list of basic beliefs held by most Jews.

Christianity and Islam are built upon the foundation of Judaism. There are too many denominations and subgroups of Christianity to consider in this chapter. However, the viewpoints by Donald E. Miller and Bob George are helpful in describing two general tendencies in Christianity. Liberal Christianity, according to Miller, is a type of Christianity which seeks to be more up-to-date, socially sensitive, and flexible. Conservative Christianity, according to George, seeks to emphasize the uniqueness of Christianity from all other religions. Liberal Christianity tends to find revelations of God's truths in many areas of life. It also tends to focus on saving society from various social evils. Conservative Christianity finds God's revelation of himself in the Bible as paramount and unique. Conservative Christianity emphasizes first bringing salvation to the individual, then working on social problems.

Islam finds its roots in the life and teaching of Muhammad. The Prophet Muhammad used the traditions of Judaism and Christianity, but ultimately rejected these traditions. He taught that the purest and final revelation of God is in the Quran (or Koran), the sacred text of Islam. Hazrat Mirza Ghulam Ahmad briefly explains three levels of life available to humans. The highest level is complete union with and submission to God (or Allah).

Two religions which developed in India and which have shaped the lives of large numbers of people are Hinduism and Buddhism. Nancy Wilson Ross explains that Hinduism is a collection of many religious beliefs, many conceptions of the divine, and many traditions. Beyond the complexity there is a common belief in Brahman, an ultimate reality which lends meaning and order to the disorder of our daily lives. There is also "Karma," the idea that one must accept what is and not fight against reality. A sense of relaxing and finding peace is also central to Buddhism. Gill Farrer-Halls explains that Buddhism is a religion of meditation, inner wisdom, and self-discipline. In contrast to Judaism, Christianity, or Islam, Buddhism is not founded on a revelation from God or even on the idea of a god. Buddhism is much more a lifestyle in which inner peace is sought.

Humanism is the last viewpoint discussed in this chapter. Corliss Lamont explains that while some humanists view their beliefs as a type of religion, many do not. More important than the question of whether or not humanism is a religion, is the thrust of humanism. Lamont explains that humanism denies the existence of the supernatural (gods, miracles, divine revelation, etc.). Instead, humanism emphasizes human development (individually and socially) and the importance of science, democracy, and individual rights.

"Judaism is a way of life that endeavors to transform virtually every human action into a means of communion with God."

Judaism Is a Life of Communing with God

Louis Finkelstein

Louis Finkelstein (1895–1991) was a leader of Judaism in America throughout most of the twentieth century. He was invited to the White House by several American presidents. He served as a professor and as chancellor at the Jewish Theological Seminary. One of his many scholarly publications was his two-volume work, *The Jews: Their History, Culture, and Religion*. In this viewpoint, Finkelstein writes that Judaism is a way of life in which people seek to obey God in every area of their lives. The will of God is first of all found in the Law given to Moses, but Finkelstein explains that the Law is explained and applied to life with the help of thousands of years of oral and written interpretations.

As you read, consider the following questions:
1. What is the Torah, and what is the Talmud?
2. According to Finkelstein, how does a person become a Jew? How does a person stop being a Jew?
3. According to Finkelstein, how do Reform, Orthodox, and Conservative Jews differ?

J udaism is a way of life that endeavors to transform virtually every human action into a means of communion with
God. Through this communion with God, the Jew is en-
abled to make his contribution to the establishment of the
Kingdom of God and the brotherhood of men on earth. So
far as its adherents are concerned, Judaism seeks to extend
the concept of right and wrong to every aspect of their behavior. Jewish rules of conduct apply not merely to worship,
ceremonial, and justice between man and man, but also to
such matters as philanthropy, personal friendships and kind-
nesses, intellectual pursuits, artistic creation, courtesy, the
preservation of health, and the care of diet.[1]

Jewish Law

So rigorous is this discipline, as ideally conceived in Jewish
writings, that it may be compared to those specified for
members of religious orders in other faiths. A casual conversation or a thoughtless remark may, for instance, be considered a grave violation of Jewish Law. It is forbidden, as a
matter not merely of good form but of religious law, to use
obscene language, to rouse a person to anger, or to display
unusual ability in the presence of the handicapped. The ceremonial observances are equally detailed. The ceremonial
Law expects each Jew to pray thrice every day, if possible at
the synagogue; to recite a blessing before and after each
meal; to thank God for any special pleasure, such as a curious sight, the perfume of a flower, or the receipt of good
news; to wear a fringed garment about his body; to recite
certain passages from Scripture each day; and to don *tephillin*
(cubical receptacles containing certain biblical passages)
during the morning prayers.

Decisions regarding right and wrong under given conditions are not left for the moment, but are formulated with
great care in the vast literature created by the Jewish religious teachers. At the heart of this literature are the Hebrew

---

1. Without desiring to ascribe to them any responsibility for this statement, the
author records with deep gratitude the assistance in its preparation given by
colleagues from different schools of Jewish thought. These include Rabbis Max
Arzt, Ben Zion Bokser, Samuel S. Cohon, Judah Goldin, Israel M. Goldman,
Simon Greenberg, David de Sola Pool, Samuel Schulman, and Aaron J. Tofield.

Scriptures, usually described as the Old Testament, consisting of the Five Books of Moses (usually called the *Torah*), the Prophets and the Hagiographa. These works, particularly the Five Books of Moses, contain the prescriptions for human conduct composed under Divine inspiration. The ultimate purpose of Jewish religious study is the application of the principles enunciated in the Scriptures, to cases and circumstances the principles do not explicitly cover.

Because Judaism is a way of life, no confession of faith can by itself make one a Jew. Belief in the dogmas of Judaism must be expressed in the acceptance of its discipline rather than in the repetition of a verbal formula. But no failure either to accept the beliefs of Judaism or to follow its prescriptions is sufficient to exclude from the fold a member of the Jewish faith. According to Jewish tradition, the covenant between God and Moses on Mt. Sinai included all those who were present and also all their descendants. . . . There is therefore no need for any ceremony to admit a Jewish child into the faith of Judaism. Born in a Jewish household, he becomes at once "a child of the covenant." The fact that the child has Jewish parents involves the assumption of the obligations that God has placed on these parents and their descendants. . . .

Judaism and Government

Like other religions, Judaism can be, and indeed has been, practiced under various forms of civil government: monarchical, semi-monarchical, feudal, democratic, and totalitarian. Adherents of the Jewish faith, like those of other religions, regard themselves as citizens or subjects of their respective states. In every synagogue prayers are offered for the safety of the government of the country of its location; and in the ancient Temple of Jerusalem daily sacrifices were offered on behalf of the imperial Roman government, as long as Palestine remained under its dominion. This patriotic loyalty to the state has often persisted in the face of cruel persecution. The principle followed has been that formulated by the ancient teacher, Rabbi Haninah: "Pray for the welfare of the government; for without fear of the government, men would have swallowed each other up alive."

Despite this ability to adjust itself to the exigencies of any form of temporal government, Judaism, like other faiths derived from the Prophets, has always upheld the principles of the Fatherhood of God and the dignity and worth of man as the child and creature of God; and its ideals are more consistent with those of democracy than any other system of government.

The most vigorous and consistent effort to formulate the discipline of Judaism in terms of daily life was that made in ancient Palestine and Babylonia. The Palestinian schools devoted to this purpose were founded in the second or third century before the Common Era, and flourished in their original form for six centuries and in a somewhat altered form until the Crusades. The Babylonian schools were founded in the third century of the Common Era and ended the first and most significant phase of their activity about three hundred years later.[2]

The rules of conduct worked out in the discussion of these academies form the substance of Jewish Law. In arriving at these precepts, the ancient teachers were guided by their desire to know the Will of God. So far as possible they sought to discover His will through an intensive study of the Scriptures. Where Scripture offered no clear guidance, they tried to ascertain His will by applying its general principles of moral right. In addition, they had a number of oral traditions, going back to antiquity, which they regarded as supplementary to the written Law, and equal to it in authority and inspiration.

The high purpose of the discussions made them of monumental importance to Judaism. As a result, they were committed to memory by eager and faithful disciples, until the memorized materials grew to such proportions that it had to be reduced to writing. The work in which the discussions were thus preserved is known as the Talmud. . . .

The Place of Study in Judaism

It is impossible to understand Judaism without an appreciation of the place it assigns to the study and practice of the tal-

2. Cf. Judah Goldin, "The Period of the Talmud (135 B.C.E.–1035 C.E.)," this work, Vol. I, Chap. 3, *passim.*

mudic Law. Doing the Will of God is the primary spiritual concern of the Jew. Therefore, to this day, he must devote considerable time not merely to the mastery of the content of the Talmud, but also to training in its method of reasoning. The study of the Bible and the Talmud is thus far more than a pleasing intellectual exercise, and is itself a means of communication with God. According to some teachers, this study is the highest form of such communion imaginable.[3]

Defining God

God said to Moses, "I AM WHO I AM. This is what you are to say to the Israelites: 'I AM has sent me to you.'"

God also said to Moses, "Say to the Israelites, 'The LORD, the God of your fathers—the God of Abraham, the God of Isaac and the God of Jacob—has sent me to you.' This is my name forever, the name by which I am to be remembered from generation to generation.

The Bible, Exodus 3:14–15, New International Version, 1973, 1978.

Because the preservation of the Divine will regarding human conduct is basic to all civilization, none of the commandments is more important than that of studying and teaching the Law. The most sacred object in Judaism is the Scroll containing the Five Books of Moses. Every synagogue must contain at least one copy of it. The Scroll must be placed in a separate Ark, before which burns an eternal light. The position of this Ark in the synagogue is in the direction of Jerusalem; everyone turns toward the Ark in prayer. When the Scroll is taken from the Ark for the purpose of reading, all those present must rise. No irreverent or profane action may be performed in a room which contains a Scroll, nor may a Scroll be moved from place to place except for the performance of religious rites. From time to time the Scroll must be examined to ascertain that its writing is intact. . . .

No less important than this homage paid to the Scroll as symbol of the Law, is that paid to the living Law itself. Fully three-fourths of the Hebrew literature produced within the

3. Cf. the essay on "Study as a Mode of Worship," by Professor Nathan Isaacs, in *The Jewish Library*, edited by Rabbi Leo Jung, 1928, pp. 51–70.

first nineteen centuries of the Common Era, is devoted to the elucidation of the Law. Many of the best minds in Judaism have been devoted to its study. Every parent is required to teach his child its basic elements. Its study is considered vital not only for the guidance it offers in the practice of Judaism, but for liberation from the burden of secular ambition and anxieties. The study of the Law is believed to be a foretaste of the immortal life, for the Sages of the Talmud believed that Paradise itself could offer men no nearer communion with God than the opportunity of discovering His will in the study of the Law.

The Talmud derives its authority from the position held by the ancient academies. The teachers of those academies, both of Babylonia and of Palestine, were considered the rightful successors of the older Sanhedrin, or Supreme Court, which before the destruction of Jerusalem (in the year 70 of the Common Era) was the arbiter of Jewish Law and custom. The Sanhedrin derived its authority from the statement in Deut. 17:8–13, that whenever a question of interpretation of the Law arises, it is to be finally decided by the Sages and priests in Jerusalem.

The Role of Rabbis

At the present time, the Jewish people have no living central authority comparable in status to the ancient Sanhedrin or the later academies. Therefore any decision regarding the Jewish religion must be based on the Talmud, as the final resume of the teachings of those authorities when they existed. The right of an individual to decide questions of religious Law depends entirely on his knowledge of the Bible, the Talmud, and the later manuals based on them, and upon his fidelity to their teachings. Those who have acquired this knowledge are called rabbis. There is no sharp distinction in religious status between the rabbi and the layman in Judaism. The rabbi is simply a layman especially learned in Scripture and Talmud. Nor is there any hierarchical organization or government among the rabbis of the world. Yet some rabbis, by virtue of their special distinction in learning, by common consent come to be regarded as superior authorities on questions of Jewish Law. Difficult and complicated issues are referred to them for clarification.

To be recognized as a rabbi, a talmudic student customarily is ordained. Traditionally, the authority to act as rabbi may be conferred by any other rabbi. It is usual, however, for students at various theological schools to receive this authority from their teachers. In America, there are several rabbinical schools, each of which ordains its graduates in the manner in which degrees are conferred on graduates of other institutions of learning. . . . There is considerable variation among the interpretations of Judaism taught at these seminaries, and consequently there is a considerable difference in emphasis on the subjects included in their respective curricula. This has resulted from the fact that during the second half of the nineteenth century various groups of rabbis, primarily in Germany and America, claimed authority not merely to interpret but also to amend talmudic, and even biblical Law. These rabbis are known as Reform rabbis, and their congregations as Reform congregations. Of the rabbis who adhere to traditional Judaism, some reject any significant innovations from customary practice; these rabbis are called Orthodox. Others maintain that Jewish law is a living tradition, subject to change, but they insist that such changes must be made in accordance with traditional canons for the interpretation and development of Rabbinic law. These rabbis are usually called Conservative.[4]

The difference between the various groups of American rabbis have not led to any sectarian schism. Although the difference in practice between the traditional and Reform groups is considerable, each accepts the other as being within the fold of Judaism. It is possible for them to do so, because of the principle that even an unobservant or a heretical Jew does not cease to be a member of the covenant made between God and Israel at the time of the Revelation. Only actual rejection of Judaism, by affiliation with another faith, is recognized as separating one from the Jewish community. So long as a follower of the Jewish faith has not by overt act or word and of his own free will declared himself a

4. For a survey of the Orthodox, Conservative, and Reform movements in the United States, see Moshe Davis, *Jewish Religious Life and Institutions in America (A Historical Study)*, pp. 310 f., 326 f.

member of another religion, other Jews are bound to regard him as one of their own faith, and to seek his return to its practice and beliefs. . . .

The Basic Concepts of Judaism

The central doctrine of Judaism is the belief in the One God, the Father of all mankind. The first Hebrew words a Jewish child learns are the confession of faith contained in the verse "Hear, O Israel, the Lord is our God, the Lord is One," and every believing Jew hopes that as he approaches his end in the fullness of time he will be sufficiently conscious to repeat this same confession. This monotheistic belief is subject to no qualification or compromise. . . .

Delighting in the Law of God

Blessed is the man
   who does not walk in the counsel
     of the wicked
or stand in the way of sinners
   or sit in the seat of mockers.
But his delight is in the law of the
     LORD,
   and on his law he meditates day
     and night.
He is like tree planted by
     streams of water,
   which yields its fruit in season
and whose leaf does not wither.
   Whatever he does prospers.

The Bible, Psalm 1:1–3, New International Version, 1973, 1978.

There is a wide variety of interpretation among Rabbinical scholars, both ancient and modern, with regard to the concepts of Judaism. In some instances, the differences of interpretation are so great that it is difficult to speak of a concept as being basically or universally Jewish or Rabbinic. There are thus a number of concepts, each having its own limited authority and following.

This applies also to a degree to the fundamental beliefs which have been brought together in the best known Jewish creed, that of Maimonides. According to this creed, there are thirteen basic dogmas in Judaism. They are as follows:

1. The belief in God's existence.
2. The belief in His unity.
3. The belief in His incorporeality.
4. The belief in His timelessness.
5. The belief that He is approachable through prayer.
6. The belief in prophecy.
7. The belief in the superiority of Moses to all other prophets.
8. The belief in the revelation of the Law, and that the Law as contained in the Pentateuch is that revealed to Moses.
9. The belief in the immutability of the Law.
10. The belief in Divine providence.
11. The belief in Divine justice.
12. The belief in the coming of the Messiah.
13. The belief in the resurrection and human immortality.

"Although Scripture and tradition are important, the basepoint of liberal morality has been reason."

Liberal Christianity Finds Many Ways to Seek God

Donald E. Miller

Donald E. Miller teaches religion, particularly from a sociological perspective, at the University of Southern California. He has also published books dealing with ethics, social issues (such as homelessness), and genocide. In this viewpoint, Miller explains that too many people feel pushed to either accept conservative, evangelical Christianity or secularism (the complete rejection of all religion). Miller argues that a third, and better, alternative is liberal Christianity.

As you read, consider the following questions:
1. According to Miller, what are some of the ways a person might grow spiritually?
2. How does Miller compare liberal Christianity and conservative Christianity?
3. Miller explains that liberal Christianity is a positive middle position between the extremes of secularism and evangelical Christianity. What do you think? What other choices exist?

Excerpted from pages 32–42 of *The Case for Liberal Christianity*, by Donald E. Miller. Copyright © 1981 by Donald E. Miller. Reprinted by permission of HarperCollins Publishers, Inc.

One of the central facts of contemporary existence is the diversity of meaning systems that individuals follow. Liberal Christianity is one framework of meaning and values. In addition to being unique as a religious framework—as opposed to a strictly secular framework, which makes no reference to things sacred, or to a transcendent reference point for evaluating the meaningfulness of human existence—liberal Christianity is distinctive insofar as it is one of several perspectives within the Christian religious framework. . . .

Defining Liberal Christianity

Liberal Christians differ from their more conservative counterparts at a number of points, but let me begin with their *view toward culture*. Rather than perceiving culture, particularly science and the arts, as a potential threat to religious faith, liberal Christians have understood that Christianity must evolve and adapt itself—or at least its expression—from age to age. They have believed that the application of the gospel must be reinterpreted from each new cultural context. Although there may be a core essence to Christianity, liberal Christians view accommodation to culture as necessary and positive, if what one means by "accommodation" is that they should seek to understand God and their moral responsibility in terms of the best available scientific knowledge and social analysis.

The Arts and Education

Liberal Christians look upon the arts as important expressions of the problems and tensions of their culture. Liberal Christians also recognize the invaluable moral critiques found in many artistic expressions. Whereas film, theater, and dance may be shunned by many conservative Christians, liberal Christians look to these artistic productions as important occasions for not only self-reflection, but also a potential uplifting and enlivening of the human spirit. Liberal Christians have long recognized that things ultimate and real can be portrayed through a variety of mediums. Thus, an evening spent reading a novel, viewing a theatrical production, or seeing a movie may be as illuminating as a comparable period of time spent reading the Bible. Liberal Christians believe that revelations may come in many forms.

Liberals have long been champions of education. They find that nothing is to be feared in knowledge. To discover the relativity of cultures is not a new insight so much as it is a foundation stone on which liberalism rests. Liberal clergy have usually been highly educated. The task implicit in sermon preparation by liberal clergy has been to blend creatively the "old gospel" with the personal, social, and political problems felt by those in the pew. As a result, psychological, sociological, and philosophical insights often have found their way into the text of sermons given by the liberal clergy. Book discussion groups have been at least as common in liberal churches as Bible study groups and prayer meetings.

The danger in liberalism is that the Christian message may become a mirror reflection of the spirit of the age. This is an ever-present problem for liberal Christians to confront. On the other hand, liberals have protested that one cannot possibly critique culture without understanding it. . . .

Morality

Liberal Christians have always placed considerable emphasis upon the moral witness of their faith. Rooted in the Social Gospel Movement of the last several decades of the nineteenth century and the first three decades of the twentieth century, liberal Christianity has always sought to apply its Gospel to the social betterment of the human community. Political rallies and social action committee meetings have often taken the place of more traditionally pious activities. In its earlier period, liberalism was married to the spirit of socialism. As political winds changed, so did the social ethic of liberal Christianity. Under the pressure of the Neo-orthodox Movement, many liberals were forced into a greater acknowledgment of the reality of sin and of the necessity of a new found political realism. Whatever the ideology, however, liberal Christians have always found themselves in the streets, politicking city councils, writing letters to congressmen, and busying themselves with social welfare concerns. Their approach stands in contrast to that of many conservative Christians who have sought to change the world by changing hearts (through conversion).

Although Scripture and tradition are important, the base-point of liberal morality has been reason. This emphasis, of course, has coincided nicely with the commitment of liberal Christians to education. In contrast to the scriptural "proof-texting" of many conservative Christians, liberals have often appealed to the broader principles of justice and love as explicated in the Bible. Reason has always been the mediating force in applying these biblical insights to particular situations. Not infrequently liberals have endorsed a contextual or situational ethic. They have been relatively inhospitable, on the other hand, to moral legalisms. Always reason is to be used in weighing the authority of Scripture and tradition. . . .

Another identifying mark of the moral commitment of liberal Christians is that they have characteristically given at least as much attention to social morality as personal morality. Matters of sexual practice and personal vice have been of interest to liberal Christians, but programmatic emphases have more typically been related to issues of war, poverty, racial discrimination, employment practices, and so forth. Systemic and social-structural problems have been understood to be at the root of much of the suffering and misery in the world. For this reason, the prophets of the Old Testament have often been appealed to as frequently as the teachings of Jesus.

Scripture

Liberal Christians differ from conservative Christians in that they generally approach Scripture nondogmatically. Liberal biblical scholars tend to apply historical, sociological, and even psychological tools and insights to their interpretations of Scripture. The hermeneutical principle often applied is that everything—Scripture included—is written within a cultural context. Therefore, to understand the meaning of a document, one must understand how and why it was written. One must also understand the world view of the writer. For example, one of the most famous biblical scholars, Rudolf Bultmann, believed that the New Testament was written from the perspective of a prescientific cosmology of a three-tiered universe (with heaven above, hell or the underworld below, and the earth, on which men and women dwell, as a mediating structure between the two). His task of demythologization was an effort to get at the kerygma (message) which lay behind this first century world view.

When the Scriptures are understood as human documents, they then are susceptible to all the canons of modern historical and literary analysis. To the liberal theologian, there is a considerable difference between viewing the Bible primarily through the eyes of faith and being equally open to a cultural and historical perspective. Historically, the resurrection of Jesus and the virgin birth are at best ambiguous as concrete occurrences. From the perspective of faith, however, they may have quite a different significance. But one should never conclude that the Scriptures are unimportant for the liberal Christian. Quite the contrary, they are central to the Christian faith. The fact that more attention is given to them as symbolic documents than as historical documents does not distort their importance.

The Bible Is Not God

Biblical literalists are always first-rate candidates for atheism. For their God, of course, is actually the Bible. And although the Bible is holy and good, it is not God. Therefore, when faith in their god, the Bible, is in any way shaken, then, like the "intelligent young man named Jitterly," they may "reject the whole thing bitterly." In the meantime, their narrow and shallow interpretation of the Bible may also cause a lot of other folks to reject it as well.

Robert Short, *Something to Believe In*, 1978.

After all, liberal Christianity (as well as fundamentalist Christianity) is based upon a message whose inspiration is taken from the life and teachings of Jesus. Whatever accommodations are to be made in applying Christianity to the contemporary setting, the liberal Christian is nevertheless compelled to go back to the rather radical teachings of Jesus concerning the kingdom. Any compromises to be made with the Sermon on the Mount, for example, are self-consciously made by understanding the setting in which Jesus was teaching and living. Likewise, any alterations of Paul's teachings on women are made, again, from the basis of an interpretation of Paul's social setting. Liberal Christians, by their very approach to Scripture, are spared the agony experienced by many conservatives who are forced, when they disagree with some biblical dictum on the grounds of social conscience, to go through what has been aptly described as a sort of "hermeneutical ventriloquism."

A basic distinction to be drawn between liberal and conservative Christians concerns the issue of God's self-declaration to man. Most conservative Christians begin with the assumption that man exists as the creation of God, a supernatural being who is personal and therefore interested in communicating with his creation. Following on this assumption, conservative Christians postulate that God has revealed himself in time and space at a number of historical junctures, the most important being his decision to give earthly form to his son, Jesus. Jesus, then, is viewed as God's clearest self-declaration of who he is. Furthermore, conservative Christians postulate that God safeguarded his self-declaration by inspiring the writers of the Bible, giving them the very words to say (or, some would argue, only the thoughts were given—while others more liberal, but still within the conservative camp, would argue that God gave official sanction to what was penned by the biblical writers).

Liberal Christians, on the other hand, tend to see the above progression as much too anthropomorphic. Even the father-son imagery seems like a projection. Rather than starting with God, postulating divine initiative, many liberal Christians begin with the human predicament and emphasize *man's search* for God. According to this approach, from the standpoint of a functional definition, God is synonymous with the search for human wholeness, for confidence in the ultimate meaningfulness of human existence. Paul Tillich's definition of faith as the *state* of Ultimate Concern is representative of the liberal perspective because the emphasis is placed upon man's search for God.

Tillich's definition of God, too, is representative of the liberal position. God is the "God above God"—meaning that man's finite limitations forever leave man short of defining in any absolute way who God is. Nevertheless, to the extent that one dares to venture a definition, it is an expansive one: God is the very "Ground of Being"; God is "Being-Itself." These definitions are nonreductive. If liberals have a central objection to the view many conservative Christians pose of God, it is that the conservative view reduces God to understandable, human terms—or human projections. Tillich's view of God as the "Ground of Being" is in reaction to that first century cosmological perspective which put God up in the sky, sitting on a throne, looking down on his creation.

Liberal Christians have viewed God in a much more immanentistic fashion. God is within creation. He is the life-force. He is at the center of all change, all innovation, all creativity. He is the source of life and is experienced in those profound moments of joy, communion, celebration. God is the "Thou" of the I-Thou encounter. He is the Ground of Being. God is present in all those activities which unite people rather than divide them, which call upon persons to transcend self-interest through brotherhood and sisterhood. God is personal as we discover our own humanity and act in his name to realize community: that state in which we relate to others as "ends" and not "means" to self-centered purposes.

The finer expressions about God in the liberal tradition have not, however, made God totally immanent. While many liberal Christians may have moved toward a healthy mysticism in both their experience and their speech about God, they have maintained the tension between God as transcendant and God as immanent. In other words, they have recognized, above all, that it is idolatrous to reduce God to human standards. He is present within his creation, he is the source of all meaning, he is at the center of all ethical structures, and yet he stands above and outside that which is purely human as the judge of all human projects. He is the "I am" of the Old Testament. He is one to both fear and worship. . . .

Symbolic Realism

Sociologist Robert Bellah has identified an important distinction between two types of "realism" that separate conservatives from liberals. Conservatives tend to be "historical realists" to the extent that they believe the truth of Christianity is found in the historical acts witnessed to in the New Testament—such as literal miracles, a literal bodily resurrection, and so forth. Historical realists are interested in understanding history "as it was." They take a nonmetaphorical and nonfigurative approach to interpreting Scripture. . . . Hence, one is "saved" if one believes that the Bible is the inspired word of God, that Jesus is the literal son of God sent down to earth to atone for mankind's sins, that he died on the cross and three days later was miraculously raised from the dead, and that he presently lives with God, sitting at his right hand.

Today's Liberal Christian

Now I hold, as do many liberal Christians today, that a Christian does not have to accept those philosophical and theological theories of the third and fourth centuries. I think that we can base our Christianity upon Jesus' teachings concerning the reality and love and claim of God, and upon the love ethic that has developed out of it. This provides a framework for life regardless of how much or how little detail we know for sure about Jesus' life.

John Hick, *Free Inquiry*, Fall 1985.

The liberal "symbolic realists," in contrast, emphasize that "meaning" is always a product of the interaction between subject and object. Meaning is *granted* to events—it is not considered inherent in them. According to this view, the Scriptures contain the record of men's and women's reflections regarding the *meaning* which Christ had *for them*. It is not primarily an historical account. The resurrection, the miracles, the virgin birth are valued as symbols that point beyond the historical event to a larger and more ultimate truth. But the truth does not lie in the symbols (as historical events). Symbols are irreducible. They are not identical with actual events, although they may derive from them. To take symbols literally is to engage in idolatry. Symbolic realists have given up hope of discovering what "really happened"; indeed, most of them are not even convinced that such knowledge would make much difference.

The symbols that surround the life of Christ—parables, stories, sayings, etc.—are understood by liberal Christians to be vitally important. It is through the symbol of Christ (which is a complex symbol, indeed) that men and women may come to know God. The symbolic form of Christ, as presented in the Gospel accounts, however, points beyond any purely historical events to a transcendent Truth or Reality (which we symbolize as God)—this is the hope and faith of liberal Christians. . . .

Conclusion

It is my opinion that what is needed in the churches today is a widescale recovery of the liberal spirit. . . .

Our social situation is ripe for a rebirth of Christian liberalism. But the ethical perspective of liberalism is only one reason for the return. Even more persuasive, in my view, is the fact that Christendom has become polarized. With a burgeoning population of evangelicals on one side and radical secularists on the other, the *mediating position. I would say, the temperate alternativ*e—of liberalism is being lost. Many young people today are unaware that there even is an option to the left of evangelicalism. And for many secularists, particularly young people, the only alternative to evangelicalism—if one wants to be religious—is membership with the "Moonies" or the Hare Krishna cult. . . .

In my view, liberalism is the most viable mode for reasserting the value of the Christian perspective to contemporary culture.

"*Christianity stands alone, separate from the world's religions, because of its unique combination of the astounding claims of the man Jesus of Nazareth and its pinpointing of those claims at a concrete place and time in history.*"

Conservative Christianity Is a Biblical Relationship with God

Bob George

Bob George has written several books which seek to make Christianity more understandable to popular audiences. He is head of a counseling organization and host of a radio talk-show where he advises those who call in. In this viewpoint, George explains conservative Christianity. He begins by stating that Christianity is rooted in historical facts. George adds that true Christianity requires both humility before God and enlightenment from God. In contrast to those thinkers who believe that there are many ways of discovering God, George writes that the Bible is the only source of truth about God.

As you read, consider the following questions:

1. Why, according to George, is Christianity unique from other religions?
2. Why does George emphasize the historical truth of the Bible?
3. George writes that some people know the Bible, but have "cold hearts." What does George mean by this? What is his solution to this problem?

Excerpted from *Growing in Grace*, by Bob George. Copyright © 1997 by Harvest House Publishers, Eugene, OR 97402. Used with permission.

Christianity stands alone, separate from the world's religions, because of its unique combination of the astounding claims of the man Jesus of Nazareth and its pinpointing of those claims at a concrete place and time in history. For example, there have been many other religious teachers in history, such as Confucius, Buddha, and Muhammad, but none of these (nor any other man) ever claimed to be God and also convinced a significant number of followers that he actually was God.

Though people throughout the ages have believed in many different gods, these were known only through vague legends and myths. No one claimed to have personally known Zeus or Thor, for example. In the world's religions you either find a historical religious teacher who claimed to know a way to successful living but was a normal man nonetheless, or else you find fanciful stories of gods and other supernatural beings who lived no one knows where or when.

The Bible and History

However, when you turn to the Bible you find a relentless presentation of objective, historical facts. Persons, places, and times are concrete. Caesar Augustus, "while Quirinius was governor of Syria" (Luke 2:2),[1] ordered a census of the empire, "so Joseph also went up from the town of Nazareth in Galilee to Judea, to Bethlehem'" (Luke 2:4). John the Baptist, the forerunner of Christ, began his ministry "in the fifteenth year of the reign of Tiberius Caesar" (Luke 3:1). Within a few weeks after Jesus' crucifixion, Peter was proclaiming in that very city of Jerusalem, "God has raised this Jesus to life, and *we are all witnesses of the fact*" (Acts 2:32). Throughout the following decades we see the message of Christ spreading like wildfire, fanned by the conviction that "we cannot help speaking about *what we have seen and heard*" (Acts 4:20). The most violent persecutor of Christians, Saul of Tarsus, is converted and later explains, "He appeared *to me* also" (1 Corinthians 15:7). With lightning speed, especially considering that this was a day without television, radio, or printing press, Christians are found throughout the

1. All biblical references are taken from the New International version of the Bible.

Roman Empire. When the last remaining eyewitness writes his account he closes with "This is the disciple who testifies to these things and who wrote them down" (John 21:24).

Right in the middle of all this solid historical setting, as the cause and center of it all, is a man who claimed to be God!

Born of the Spirit

In reply Jesus declared, "I tell you the truth, no one can see the kingdom of God unless he is born again."

"How can a man be born when he is old?" Nicodemus asked. "Surely he cannot enter a second time into his mother's womb to be born!"

Jesus answered, "I tell you the truth, no one can enter the kingdom of God unless he is born of water and the Spirit. Flesh gives birth to flesh, but the Spirit gives birth to spirit.

The Bible, John 3:3–6, New International Version, 1973, 1978.

These things are not the result of blind faith or some emotional leap. They are presented as facts that are either true or are not. For almost 20 centuries, millions of men and women have examined these claims, have come to the conclusion that Jesus Christ is indeed alive and that He is Lord, and have entered into a personal relationship with Him. This is the foundation of our faith. It is rational, intelligent, and open to investigation. This brings me back to my main point: If we want to discover the real meaning and experience of "Christ in you," we must learn to take this same objective, clear-thinking faith that forms the foundation of Christianity and bring it into our daily lives. *Only in this way will we ever grow in grace.* The Jesus who made those claims almost 2000 years ago is now glorified and exalted at the Father's right hand, and He is the same living Christ who lives in and through us today through the indwelling Holy Spirit.

During His earthly ministry Jesus Christ continually pointed people to the Scriptures, the *written* Word that testified about Him, the *living* Word. In His criticism of the Pharisees He said, "If you believed Moses, you would believe Me, for he wrote about Me" (John 5:46). When He walked with the two disciples on the way to Emmaus after His resurrection, He challenged their despondent attitudes and said that it resulted from their unbelief.

> He said to them, "How foolish you are, and how slow of
> heart to believe all that the prophets have spoken! Did not
> the Christ have to suffer these things and then enter his
> glory?" And beginning with Moses and all the Prophets, He
> explained to them what was said in all the Scriptures *concern-
> ing Himself* (Luke 24.25–27).

Later, after appearing to His disciples in His resurrected
form, He said to them:

> "This is what I told you while I was still with you: Everything
> must be fulfilled that is *written about Me* in the Law of Moses,
> the Prophets and the Psalms." Then He opened their minds
> so they could understand the Scriptures (Luke 24:44,45).

True Understanding of the Bible

It was necessary for Christ to open their minds, and to show
them that the Scriptures, like history, are "His story." Today,
He must open *our* minds before we can correctly understand
the *meaning* of God's Word. First Corinthians 2:14 tells us,
"The man without the Spirit does not accept the things that
come from the Spirit of God, for they are foolishness to him,
and he cannot understand them, because they are spiritually
discerned." A true knowledge of Christ and His Word does
not come through human intelligence, intellectual ability, or
mere study. God says, "No eye has seen, no ear has heard, no
mind has conceived what God has prepared for those who
love Him" (1 Corinthians 2:9). How then can we discover
the true knowledge of Christ? "God has revealed it to us by
His Spirit" (1 Corinthians 2:10). That is exactly why you
find so often in Paul's letters passages like this:

> For this reason, ever since I heard about your faith in the
> Lord Jesus and your love for all the saints, I have not stopped
> giving thanks for you, remembering you in my prayers. I
> keep asking that the God of our Lord Jesus Christ, the glo-
> rious Father, *may give you the Spirit of wisdom and revelation,
> so that you may know Him better.* I pray also that *the eyes of your
> heart may be enlightened* in order that you may know the hope
> to which He has called you, the riches of His glorious inher-
> itance in the saints, and His incomparably great power for us
> who believe (Ephesians 1:15–19).

Notice that wisdom and revelation are gifts from God,
not learned attributes. Who does God give these gifts to?

"God opposes the proud, but *gives grace to the humble*" (James 4:6). Recognition of who *Christ* is—God—and who *we* are—God's creation—demands a response of dependency from any intelligent, thinking person. However, our dependency on Christ is something of a paradox. On one hand, we need the written Word as our objective standard of truth; but on the other hand, we must live in dependence upon the Spirit of God to open our minds to a spiritual understanding beyond knowing mere words of ink on paper. God does not reveal truth *contrary to* His written Word, but neither does He want His people to become experts in His written Word whose goal is not to know the Person of Christ who is the living Word!

If we fall into the first error, that of seeking spiritual knowledge apart from the objective truth of the Scriptures, we are left defenseless and open to all kinds of mystical nonsense and error. We will find ourselves "tossed back and forth by the waves, and blown here and there by every wind of teaching and by the cunning and craftiness of men in their deceitful scheming" (Ephesians 4:14). Several times a week I receive calls on our radio program, "People to People," from listeners in this category. It is amazing to see the kinds of error that people can fall into who have no standard or plumbline of truth! . . .

In order to worship the *true* Christ, we must be worshiping the *biblical* Christ! Any other Jesus is a figment of man's imagination, which can neither save you nor enable you to walk in the newness of His life. To "believe in" a nonbiblical Jesus is really just a form of idolatry—man's tendency to worship a god of his own creation. Only through the Scriptures can we learn absolute, authoritative truth about God, man, salvation, and life.

Study Plus a Humble Heart

But we can get off on the other side just as easily. Mere words printed on a page, knowledge of doctrines, or systematic theologies cannot satisfy the "God-shaped vacuum" in our hearts that cries out for a personal encounter with the living God. Sincere, dedicated Christians can still fall into the same error as the Pharisees, to whom Jesus said:

You diligently study the Scriptures because you think that by them you possess eternal life. *These are the Scriptures that testify about Me, yet you refuse to come to Me* to have life (John 5:39,40). . . .

All of God's truth is addressed to the humble—to people who recognize their need for grace, that they cannot understand truth on their own, that they cannot live the Christian life on their own. Proud people cannot receive grace because they *will not* receive grace. They are convinced of their own sufficiency and enamored by their own ability. Therefore they can learn the words and debate the Scriptures but still miss Christ. You can very easily have a highly trained intellect but a cold heart. . . .

In order to grow in grace we need both of these attitudes: a commitment to the Scriptures as God's revelation of truth for our lives, and a humble recognition of our dependency on the Spirit of God to empower us to know the God *of* the Scriptures.

"*The real object of man's life according to the Quran is, therefore, a true knowledge and worship of God and a total resignation to His will so that whatever is said or done is for His sake only.*"

Islam Is the Way to Obey God

Hazrat Mirza Ghulam Ahmad

Hazrat Mirza Ghulam Ahmad (1835–1908) wrote numerous books to promote the Islamic faith. Living in British Colonial India, he was a leader and teacher who sought to rationally explain the superiority of Islam to Christianity and Hinduism. Later in his life, Ahmad worked to promote a greater respect for Islam in Europe. He was called a "mujaddid," a reformer and defender of Islam. This viewpoint discusses three levels of moral development open to all humans. The third level, which is the ultimate goal of human life, is complete submission and obedience to the one true God, Allah. The author concludes by listing eight ways to seek this highest state of life.

As you read, consider the following questions:
1. According to Ahmad, humans can be motivated in three ways: by animal passions, by reason and knowledge, and by submission to God. What are the results of these motivations?
2. The author lists eight ways to totally submit to God. Does the author exclude all other ways of submitting to God?

Excerpted from *Teachings of Islam*, by Hazrat Mirza Ghulam Ahmad, translated by Maulana Muhammad Ali (Lanore, Pakistan: Ahmadiyyah Anjuman Isha'at Islam, 1910).

In the name of Allāh, the Beneficent, the Merciful—1:1. . . .

The first question relates to the physical, moral and spiritual conditions of man. The Quran observes this division by fixing three respective sources for this threefold condition of man, that is, three springs out of which these three conditions flow. The first of these in which the physical conditions of man take their birth is termed the *nafs al-ammāra*, which signifies the "uncontrollable spirit", or the "spirit prone to evil". . . .

It is characteristic of the *nafs al-ammāra* that it inclines man to evil, tends to lead him into iniquitous and immoral paths, and stands in the way of his attainment of perfection and moral excellence. Man's nature is prone to evil and transgression at a certain stage in his development, and so long as he is devoid of high moral qualities, this evil nature is predominant in him. He is subject to this state so long as he does not walk in the light of true wisdom and knowledge, but acts in obedience to the natural inclinations of eating, drinking, sleeping, becoming angry or excited, just like the lower animals.

As soon, however, as he frees himself from the control of animal passions and, guided by reason and knowledge, he holds the reins of his natural desires and governs them instead of being governed by them—when a transformation is worked in his soul from grossness to virtue—he then passes out of the physical state and is a moral being in the strict sense of the word.

The Self-Accusing Soul

The source of the moral conditions of man is called, in the terminology of the Quran, the *nafs al-lawwāma*, or the "self-accusing soul". . . .

This is the spring from which flows a highly moral life and, on reaching this stage, man is freed from bestiality. The swearing by the self-accusing soul indicates the regard in which it is held. For, the change from the disobedient to the self-accusing soul being a sure sign of its improvement and purification makes it deserving of approbation in the sight of the Almighty.

Lawwāma literally means "one who reproves severely",

and the *nafs al-lawwāma* (self-accusing soul) has been so called because it upbraids a man for the doing of evil deeds and strongly hates unbridled passions and bestial appetites. Its tendency, on the other hand, is to generate noble qualities and a virtuous disposition, to transform life so as to bring the whole course and conduct of it to moderation, and to restrain the carnal passions and sensual desires so as to keep them within due bound.

Pursuing Righteousness

On the scale of virtue and righteousness, people occupy varying positions. The scale itself is infinite; and there is no point at which Muslims may carry their titles to Paradise, as it were, in their pockets. Everyone strives and some strive more than others. God's judgment of a person's fate is not preempted by anything that an individual can do, whether for or against salvation. For God may reject the greatest deeds because of lack of faith and seriousness on the part of their doer, and He may forgive the greatest sinner. The Muslim, therefore, is a person who, having joined the ranks of Islam by solemn declaration, is engaged in the pursuit of righteousness for the rest of his or her life. Thus the simple test of "Islamicity" provided by Islamic law is balanced by a requisite for salvation which is by nature infinite and hence never fully satisfied. Religious justification is thus the Muslims' eternal hope, never their complacent certainty, not for even a fleeting moment.

Muslims, therefore, are people who, as they have solemnly declared, believe that only God is God and Muhammad is His Prophet. . . .

Isma'il R. Al Faruqi, *Islam*, 1984.

Although, as stated above, the "self-accusing soul" upbraids itself for its faults and frailties, yet it is not the master of its passions, nor is it powerful enough to practise virtue exclusively. The weakness of the flesh has the upper hand sometimes, and then it stumbles and falls down. Its weakness then resembles that of a child who does not wish to fall but whose legs are sometimes unable to support him. It does not, however, persist in its fault, every failure bringing a fresh reproach. At this stage, the soul is anxious to attain moral excellence, and revolts against disobedience which is the characteristic of the first, or the animal stage, but does, notwithstanding its yearning for virtue, sometimes deviate from the line of duty.

The Soul at Rest

The third or the last stage in the onward movement of the soul is reached on attaining to the source of all spiritual qualities. The soul at this stage is, in the words of the Quran, the *nafs al-mutma'inna*, or the "soul at rest". . . .

The soul is now freed from all weaknesses and frailties and is braced with spiritual strength. It is perfectly united with God and cannot live without Him. As water flows with great force down a slope and, on account of its great mass and the total absence of all obstacles, dashes down with irresistible force, so does the soul at this stage, casting off all trammels, flow unrestrained towards its Maker.

It is further clear from the words "O soul that art at rest with thy Lord, return to Him" that it is in this life, and not after death, that this great transformation is worked and that it is in this world, and not elsewhere, that access to paradise is granted to it. Again, as the soul has been commanded to return to its Master, it is clear that such a soul finds its support only in its Supporter. The love of God is its food, and it drinks deep at this fountain of life and is, therefore, delivered from death. . . .

The Goal of Life

The real object of man's life according to the Quran is, therefore, a true knowledge and worship of God and a total resignation to His will so that whatever is said or done is for His sake only. One thing, at least, is plain: man has no choice in the matter of fixing the aim of life. He is a creature, and the Creator, Who has brought him into existence and bestowed upon him higher and more excellent faculties than upon other animals, has also assigned an object to his existence. A man may or may not understand it, or a hundred different motives may hold him back from it, but the truth is that the grand aim of man's life consists in knowing and worshiping God and living for His sake. . . .

We are now in a position to answer the second part of the

question: how this object can possibly be attained?

The **first** means towards the attainment of this end is that, in the recognition of the Lord, a man should tread upon the right path and have his faith in the true and living God. The goal can never be reached by the man who takes the first step in the wrong direction and looks upon some stone or creature or an element of nature as his deity. The true Master assists those who seek Him, but a dead deity cannot assist its dead worshippers. . . .

Basic Beliefs of Islam

Members of the *Ahmadiyyah Anjuman Iṣḥā'at Islām* (Lahore Pakistan) believe that:

—After the holy Prophet Muhammad (Peace be upon him), God has barred the appearance of any prophet, new or old.

—Angel Gabriel cannot bring 'prophetic revelation' to any person as this would contradict the two complementary verses: "This day have I perfected for you your religion" (5:3); "Muhammad is the Messenger of Allāh and the Seal of the prophets" (33:40). It would otherwise violate the sanctity of finality of prophethood in Islam.

—All the Companions of the Holy Prophet Muhammad *(aṣḥāb)* and all the spiritual leaders *(imām)* are venerable.

—It is incumbent to believe in the missions of all reformers *(mujaddid)*.

—He who believes that "there is no God but Allāh and Muhammad is His Prophet" *(kalimah)* cannot be regarded an unbeliever or infidel *(kāfir)*.

—No verse of the holy Quran has been, or shall ever be, abrogated.

Ahmadiyyah Anjuman Iṣḥā at Islām, *Teachings of Islam*, Lahore, Pakistan, n.d.

The **second** means to attain the true object of life consists in being informed of the perfect beauty which the Benefactor possesses. Beauty naturally attracts the heart and incites love. The beauty of God consists in His unity, His majesty, His grandeur and His other lofty attributes. . . .

The **third** means of reaching the goal consists in realizing the immense goodness of the Lord. . . .

The **fourth** means for the desired end is prayer. . . .

The **fifth** means is to seek God by spending one's substance and faculties, and sacrificing one's life and applying one's wisdom in His way:

> "And strive hard in Allah's way with your wealth and your lives . . ."— 9:41. . . .

The **sixth** means by which a person may safely attain to the goal is perseverance, that is, he should be indefatigable in the way in which he walks and unswerving under the hardest trial:

> "(As for) those who say, Our Lord is Allah, then continue in the right way, the angels descend upon them, saying: Fear not, nor be grieved, and receive good news of the Garden which you were promised. We are your friends in this world's life and in the Hereafter . . ."—41:30–31.

In these verses, we are told that perseverance in faith brings about the pleasure of God. It is true, as the Arabic proverb goes, that "perseverance is more than a miracle." The highest degree of perseverance is called forth when adversities encompass a man all around, when he is threatened with loss of life, property and honour in the Divine path. . . .

The **seventh** means to attain the object is to keep company with the righteous and to imitate their perfect example. . . .

The **eighth** means is true visions and revelations from God. As the path which leads to the Creator is a secret and mysterious one, and is full of difficulties and dangers, the spiritual wayfarer may depart from the right course or despair of attaining the goal. The Divine grace, therefore, continues to encourage and strengthen him in his spiritual journey, gives him consolation in moments of grief and animates him with a still more zealous desire to pursue his journey eagerly.

Such is the Divine law with the wayfarers of His path that He continues to cheer their hearts with His word and to reveal to them that He is with them! Thus strengthened, they undertake this journey with great vigour. The Holy Book says:

> "For them (the believers) is good news in this world's life and in the Hereafter."—10:64

It may be added that the Quran has described numerous other ways which assist us in reaching the goal of life, but we cannot describe them here for want of space.

> "The attainment of individual mystic union
> with the Divine Reality which exists
> eternally behind the world's ever-changing
> maya is Hinduism's highest aim."

Hinduism Explains That All Ways Lead to God

Nancy Wilson Ross

Nancy Wilson Ross has studied eastern religious thought and religious art extensively. In addition to publishing numerous books on these subjects, she has also written several novels. In this selection, Ross gives a general explanation of why Hinduism is able to tolerate, even embrace, so many different forms of worship. Yet, behind the diversity of religious forms and social classes, Ross finds unity.

As you read, consider the following questions:

1. According to Nancy Wilson Ross, how is Hinduism complex and how is it simple?
2. What is the Brahman?
3. According to this selection, what factors divide humanity and what factors unify humanity?

Excerpted from *Three Ways of Asian Wisdom: Hinduism, Buddhism, Zen, and Their Significance for the West*, by Nancy Wilson Ross (New York: Simon & Schuster). Copyright © 1966 by Nancy Wilson Ross. Reprinted by permission of Harold Ober Associates Incorporated.

Although large gatherings of devout Hindus watch priestly performances in Hindu temples, they do not constitute a congregation in the Western sense of the term; they might more accurately be called an audience. Temples are open at all times with special services held during festivals when large numbers of pilgrims and devotees gather for prayer and to make votive offerings. Daily worship in Hinduism, however, takes place in the home, where devotional procedures are each individual's personal responsibility; no priest, regardless of his hierarchical rank, can serve as another man's spiritual proxy. Of paramount importance, therefore, is an orthodox Hindu's own prescribed observance of the ritual minutiae whereby he maintains an intimate, often complicated, relationship between himself and whatever expression of Divinity he has chosen to worship from a crowded pantheon of male and female deities. Like the temple priests—and only to a slightly less demanding degree—every orthodox householder learns and practices devotional skills that might almost be classified as technical, for the complex rituals of Hindu *puja* (worship of a god by way of his image or an abstract symbol) requires expert use of fire, water, lights, scents, sounds, flowers, grasses and leaves. Priests, householders and *sadhus* (holy men) also employ in their worship a variety of meaningful postures, gestures and utterances, and it is this intense personalism and ritual intimacy that have unquestionably helped Hinduism maintain, for so many centuries, its immemorial usages.

The Complexity of Hinduism

It has been often remarked that almost all thought in India is, in a sense, "religious thought" and that the national consciousness has, for millennia, found its real fulfillment in religious activity of one sort or another. It is quite true that even in modern India conversations on spiritual matters, or religious beliefs, are considered eminently suitable, and certainly enjoyable, forms of social exchange. Yet it must be kept in mind, as stated in the Foreword to this volume, that nothing can be asserted about Hinduism that cannot also be denied. It is essential to approach even the most cursory study with extreme care in order to avoid leaping to the wrong conclusions. There is encountered in Hinduism not one single religion but a variety of popular, metaphysical and symbolic expressions spread over an immense area of humanity. On the one hand one sees the country people still living in intimate communion with some personal god chosen from among the many thousands, even millions, of deities that enliven this ancient land's rich mythology. The Hindu masses' meticulous observance of immemorial ritual, often childish and superstitious in the modern view, is balanced by the presence in Hinduism of many great teachers and disciples of a purified faith rooted in humanism and universalism. Dr. Amiya Chakravarty has pointed out an interesting fact: Down the centuries India's greatest religious leaders have all been "iconoclasts" in one way or another, and scarcely one of its many gifted scholars, philosophers, poets, saints or periodic reformers has been a "professional Brahmin" abiding by the strict behavior patterns of the hereditary sacerdotal caste.

Perhaps it is the wide range of accepted practice and credo in this long-enduring socio-religious organism that helps to account for Hinduism's absence of aggressive proselytizing force. Whatever the reason, Hinduism's history has, in general, been marked by a live-and-let-live tolerance extended to other world faiths, founded on very different interpretations of God's function in the universe, as well as to the widely divergent approaches to Divinity included within its own boundaries. The charge of heresy by which Christians, Jews and Muslims have rejected unfamiliar theological concepts has relatively little place in Hinduism, which holds that there are innumerable valid ways to serve and worship the transcendent all-pervasive One who rules the world. There have been, of course, minor persecutions among sects in the long history of Hinduism and, with the rise of the modern spirit of nationalism, the inevitable bristly antagonisms and assumptions of spiritual and cultural superiority natural to a repressed colonial people rediscovering their inherent worth. Hinduism has, however, never fostered a church militant or organized all-out crusades against infidels and unbelievers in the name of a One True Faith—nor does it seem likely that it ever will. Even the modern conflict between the post-partition Muslim state of Pakistan and the new Indian Republic appears to be, on India's side at least, more political and territorial than ideological in any religious sense, and certainly Mahatma Gandhi's remarkable pattern of behavior in the midst of the tragic internecine strife of the postwar period was considered by the vast majority of Hindus to represent an exemplary expression of true Indian ideals of tolerance and harmlessness.

The Essence of Hinduism

An ancient prayer widely used in India petitions that the individual be led from illusion to reality, from ignorance to knowledge, and from mortality to immortality. This prayer contains salient features of Hinduism: concern for the life of man is the chief concern; the ideal life for man is a life of progressive development; man's life is capable of tremendous expansion; from present appearances he can move to reality; his state of ignorance can be overcome; he can be freed from time-bindedness; and he may appeal to universal powers for assistance. The absence of praise or adoration of the gods ought not to pass unnoticed.

> From the unreal lead me to the real!
> From darkness lead me to light!
> From death lead me to immortality!

Troy Wilson Organ, *The Hindu Quest for the Perfection of Man*, 1970.

Although it is not altogether easy to account for Hinduism's record of permissiveness and its lack of organized missionary zeal, it seems fair to speculate that some of this tolerance has its source in the ancient Indian theory of *karma*. Karma—about which more will be said later—is in simplest terms the belief in predestination or "what is to be will be." Such a belief is bound to modify or exclude any fanatical proselytizing as it also encourages, to some degree, an attitude of passivity and acceptance that remains basic to Hinduism even though some teachings about karma suggest how man's individual destiny can be altered by the development of higher faculties. The Hindu view of the nature of time may also have played its part in minimizing conversion pressures. Time, for Hindus, does not move, as in Western thought, from past through present to future. Instead it swings eternally, like the seasons, in immense cycles, forever recurring, waxing and waning. In such a scheme of endless periodicity final goals are bound to be more abstract than the type of destination basic to belief in such relatively static, not so remote futures as the Heavens and Hells of the Christians, Jews and Muslims.

Sacred Literature

Unlike Christianity, Islam, or that other great India-born religion, Buddhism, Hinduism had no single founder. Its main spiritual source is traced back to a body of very ancient and anonymous "revealed scriptures," the Vedas, which in turn had their origin in even older hymns of worship sung for centuries by light-skinned Aryan nomads (common ancestors of Northern Europeans) who came into India through the Himalayan passes at about the time Moses was leading the people of Israel out of Egypt. . . .

The most ancient Vedic teachings are designated in Hinduism as *shruti* or "that which was heard." Less archaic, though also sacred, Hindu literature is described as *smriti* or "that which was remembered." The "eternal revealed" Vedas, Hinduism's primary scriptures, are four in number. Of these four the Rig Veda is generally accepted as the oldest text among the world's living religions. It is written in antique Sanskrit (which, it should be remembered, is a remote relative of most of the languages of Europe) and contains among many hymns and prayers an ancient song of worship with which countless Indians to this day greet the morning sun:

> Let us meditate upon the adorable
> Glory of the Divine Life-Giver
> And may He direct our thoughts.

The earth and higher celestial atmospheres are also mentioned in this very old hymn from mankind's infancy, along with a central spiritual source of man's intellect and divine consciousness. . . .

The Indescribable Reality

Nevertheless, and contrary to all appearances, Hinduism's seeming chaos does contain a basic universal concept: the underlying belief in one immutable, ultimate, indescribable Reality known as Brahman. . . .

Brahman, the nonpersonal Supreme One, pervades all things and transcends all things. Of this great Principle, the Rig Veda states, "Though men call it by many names, it is really One." An essential part of the teaching regarding Brahman is the belief that a man can, by personal effort, and use of inner knowledge, attain union with this Divine One while still on earth. Such blissful union is made possible because the Ultimate Reality and the individual soul (*atman*), though seemingly apart, are, in actuality, one and the same substance. This identity of soul and God in Hinduism is given terse expression in an often-quoted Sanskrit formula: *Tat tvam asi*, or "That art Thou." . . .

A Poor Struggling Soul Yearning

I am but a poor struggling soul yearning to be wholly good—wholly truthful and wholly non-violent in thought, word and deed; but ever failing to reach the ideal which I know to be true. It is a painful climb, but the pain of it is a positive pleasure to me. Each step upward makes me feel stronger and fit for the next.

I am endeavouring to see God through service of humanity, for I know that God is neither in heaven, nor down below, but in every one.

Mahatma Ghandi, *All Men Are Brothers*, 1960.

The attainment of individual mystic union with the Divine Reality which exists eternally behind the world's ever-changing maya [the world our senses experience] is Hinduism's highest aim, and it cannot be too often repeated that this belief in one supreme Divinity serves to place Hinduism among monotheistic world faiths, in spite of its bewildering acceptance, on certain levels, of devotional practices polytheistic or animistic in nature.

Hinduism's basic tolerance for bizarre or unfamiliar types of human behavior in acts of worship is curiously offset in the social realm by many strict tabus having their source in the time-honored organization of Indian society into a rigid system of castes. These contradictory traits of easy acceptance and rigid exclusiveness, so characteristic of the Hindu attitude toward life, are also outgrowths of that universal law of moral compensation already referred to as karma. The doctrine of karma is inseparably tied to the theory of reincarnation, and reincarnation in its most rudimentary interpretation is the belief that each man existed before and will exist again and again until at last he has effected his final escape from the eternal round of "becoming."

In the Hindu view, as a consequence of the operation throughout the entire universe of the inescapable karmic law of periodic return, men are to be found living at many different stages of development along a many-lived path or "process." It would therefore be sheer folly to expect everybody to approach the Divine in the same manner. An intellectual would naturally strive toward God-consciousness by way of abstract metaphysical speculation, meditation, or some of the many forms of specific spiritual disciplines known as yoga. A simple villager, on the other hand, might find it necessary to satisfy his personal religious needs with colorful childish ceremonies and the worship of images whose exaggerated number of heads and arms are simply the popular Hindu way of expressing a deity's various powers and attributes.

> "By following the Buddhist path we aim to awaken to our true nature, the enlightened qualities of a Buddha."

Buddhism Seeks the Ultimate Reality

Gill Farrer-Halls

In the following viewpoint, Gill Farrer-Halls explains the basic tenets of Buddhism. Rather than being a religion where a creator god is worshiped, it is a religion of meditation. Buddhism begins with a very strong inward focus. Once a certain level of inner strength and wisdom is achieved, the individual can begin to properly order his or her relationships with the world at large.

As you read, consider the following questions:

1. What role does faith have in Buddhism? How would you define this faith?
2. Why is meditation so important to Buddhism? How does this compare to the importance of the Bible in Christianity or the importance of the Koran in Islam?
3. What is Nirvana?

Reprinted, from *The Illustrated Encyclopedia of Buddhist Wisdom*, by Gill Farrer-Halls (Wheaton, IL: Quest Books, 2000), by permission of the publisher.

Buddhism is not a belief system or an abstract philosophy. It is a way of life, with teachings on how to behave and qualities to cultivate. Its methodology is meditation, something we practice rather than study. By following the Buddhist path we aim to awaken to our true nature, the enlightened qualities of a Buddha.

Prince Siddhartha [the founder of Buddhism] renounced all his possessions and pleasures, and we too need to develop a sense of renunciation. Luckily, this does not necessarily mean abandoning everything and living in a cave for years! Though, if this is what we choose, we are following a pure and authentic Buddhist path.

Renunciation means lessening both our attachment to those things we like and our aversion to unpleasant situations and feelings, by realizing that none of these things have an inherent ability to make us happy or unhappy.

Dealing with Desire and Aversion

As Buddhists we can still have nice things and enjoy them, but when they are taken away, we accept it and do not get upset. We try not to be greedy or to seek too hard to satisfy our desires. We can learn to live with and accept our desires without the obsession to satisfy them immediately. At the same time, we can learn to accept disagreeable things without fighting against them. We can rest in the knowledge that whatever bothers us is impermanent and will pass.

A tightly closed fist tries to grasp hold of things, but they slip away because of this grasping. If we open our hands, things pour over and move on unimpeded. In this way, by not trying to control the natural flow of life, we can enjoy it. When we loosen our grasping we become open, which makes us receptive to our environment. We can appreciate other people and our surroundings beyond our tightly held perceptions.

Everyone seeks happiness but as Shakyamuni Buddha said, "There is no way to happiness—happiness is the way." Living a life guided by compassion and wisdom will help us to find happiness in the here and now.

When we first encounter Buddha's teachings the ideas can seem so wonderful that we think being a Buddhist will make us special or different in some way. But, we should not lose sight of the ordinary; we are normal and share the same nature as all other beings. The only difference is that we have the opportunity to awaken to our buddhanature through listening to the teachings and applying them in our lives. Therefore we do not have to dress differently, or shave our heads, or appear different from others—unless we choose to become a nun or a monk.

Giving Up and Finding Peace

Submit to Nature if you would reach your goal.

For, whoever deviates from Nature's way, Nature forces back again.

Whoever gives up his desire to improve upon Nature will find Nature satisfying all his needs.

Whoever finds his desires extinguished will find more desires arising of their own accord.

Whoever desires little is easily satisfied.

Whoever desires much suffers frustration.

Therefore, the intelligent person is at one with Nature, and so serves as a model for others.

Lao Tzu, *Tao Teh King*, n.d.

Being vegetarian is an appropriate expression of the Buddha's teaching on not harming others, but it is not essential. Diet is culturally conditioned. Tibetans eat meat because it is difficult to grow vegetables in their climate. Theravada Buddhists depend on alms and therefore eat whatever they are given. Chinese Buddhists, and Buddhists in the traditions that developed from Ch'an, such as Korean, are usually strictly vegetarian.

We must each choose for ourselves whether to be vegetarian or not. Food in the West is plentiful. This has caused obsession over food, reflected in diseases like bulimia and anorexia. Buddhism emphasises a middle way approach, eating moderately, and this is perhaps most important.

Death, God, and Nirvana

Buddhism is sometimes thought to be gloomy and pessimistic because it teaches us to look at the inevitability of death. However, realizing we will die encourages us to make the most of

116

our lives. Then we investigate what Buddha said would make us happy and try to live according to his teachings.

Buddhism is not a theistic religion, and Buddha was not a creator God, as in Christianity. Nirvana is not heaven; it is a state of enlightenment that can be experienced here and now. An enlightened being—a Buddha, or Bodhisattva—can rest in Nirvana or purposefully enter the world to benefit all other beings. Thus Nirvana is not a place, it is the extinguishing of suffering, delusion, and craving.

The Three Jewels

When we commit ourselves to the Buddhist path, we first take refuge in the Three Jewels. This means relying upon them for guidance. Normally we take refuge in external objects—for example, when we are hungry we take refuge in food—but these bring only temporary satisfaction. The Buddha, Dharma, and Sangha are inner resources, and are reliable objects of refuge.

We take refuge in the Buddha because he has gone beyond suffering and developed great wisdom and compassion. Buddha has no partiality and wishes to help everyone, no matter who they are or what they have done. There are as many ways to teach people as there are human dispositions, so the Buddha can guide each individual according to need.

Refuge in the Buddha alludes to being open to and relying upon the limitless love, compassion, and wisdom of those who have attained enlightenment. It also means cultivating our own potential buddhanature, seeds of enlightenment within us.

In order to be free of suffering, we must first know what it is and understand what the causes are. This means training our minds by following the teachings. We take refuge in the Dharma, the true protection from suffering, by developing wisdom from our study and practice of the Buddha's teachings.

Refuge in the Dharma is trusting that the teachings of the Buddha will ultimately lead us to enlightenment, by following the methods he taught. It also means developing our own inner wisdom that tells us what is right and wrong.

Without inspiration from our more advanced spiritual friends and teachers, we are likely to experience many disheartening problems that make it difficult to maintain our Dharma practice and meditation. So we take refuge in the Sangha and follow their example when we have problems.

Refuge in the Sangha refers to our spiritual friends. By talking together we can share experiences, find answers to questions, and resolve problems. Meditating together is inspiring and develops faith. Refuge in the Sangha is also recognizing that we too can help our friends.

The Foundation of the Kingdom of Righteousness

(THE FIRST SERMON ASCRIBED TO GAUTAMA BUDDHA)

And the Blessed One thus addressed the five monks: "There are two extremes, monks, which he who has given up the world ought to avoid.

"What are these two extremes? A life given to pleasures, devoted to pleasures and lusts; this is degrading, sensual, vulgar, ignoble, and profitless.

"And a life given to mortifications; this is painful, ignoble, and profitless.

"By avoiding these two extremes, monks, the Tathagata has gained the knowledge of the middle path which leads to insight, which leads to wisdom, which conduces to calm, to knowledge, to Sambodhi (supreme enlightenment), to Nirvana.

"Which, monks, is this middle path the knowledge of which the Tathagata has gained, which leads to insight, which leads to wisdom, which conduces to calm, to knowledge, to Sambodhi, to Nirvana?

"It is the noble eightfold path, namely: right views, right intent, right speech, right conduct, right means of livelihood, right endeavour, right mindfulness, right meditation."

Robert O. Ballou, ed. *The Portable World Bible*, 1944.

To take refuge fully in the Three Jewels we need to cultivate two qualities of mind. We must first really wish to be free from suffering. We can think of this in terms of our current life or of not being reborn in the lower realms in future lives. We must also sincerely believe that the Three Jewels can help us. Then we have really taken refuge.

The Wheel of Life depicts how we are trapped in samsara. At the center of the Wheel are three animals, symbolic of the three poisons. They are shown head to tail eating each other, which symbolizes endless cycles of suffering, with one poison causing the next.

The pig represents ignorance, blindness, and delusion. This refers to our erroneous perception of how the world exists; we believe things exist independently and provide lasting satisfaction. We also believe that we exist concretely, rather than in dependence on our different components and external conditions.

This ignorance of how things exist leads to desire, represented by the cock. We mistakenly believe a desired object will bring us enduring happiness. So desire, craving, and lust arise, which cause us suffering, because no sooner do we get what we want than we want something else.

Unsatisfied desire leads to hatred and anger, symbolized by the snake. Because we believe ourselves to exist independently, we place fulfilling our own desires above the well-being of others. So when we don't get what we want, we feel hatred or anger toward someone who has the object we crave.

Anger and hatred prevent us from thinking clearly. So when we suffer these feelings we are unable to change our erroneous perception of how things exist, which keeps us in ignorance. . . .

Is there an end to this self-perpetuating suffering? If we look at the picture we see Buddha at the top left, standing outside the Wheel of Life pointing to the moon. He symbolizes liberation from ignorance, desire, and hatred—the causes of suffering. Taking refuge in the Three Jewels helps free us from the three poisons and the five hindrances.

The Five Hindrances

Buddha described five mental states which hinder our spiritual progress and perpetuate suffering. They are: (1) sensual desire, (2) ill will, (3) sloth and torpor, (4) worry and restlessness, and (5) confused doubt.

As well as following the Buddha's path generally, we can also apply specific remedies. For instance, if we feel overwhelming desire for another person, we can lessen our suffering by meditating on the repulsive nature of his or her body. We can visualize what the body is composed of and that it will decompose at death. We can consciously direct goodwill at someone toward whom we feel ill will. We can meditate that this person also wishes to be happy and avoid suffering, just as we do.

Sloth and torpor are best overcome by eating less and taking more exercise. Worry and restlessness often arise from an uneasy conscience, so repenting any negative actions and resolving to not do them again lessens worry. This is the purpose of Catholic confession and psychotherapy, both summed up with the saying "a problem shared is a problem halved."

Confused doubt, as opposed to skeptical questioning, which is useful, is best cured by further practice and study of Buddha's teachings. As we saw with worry, talking things over with like-minded spiritual friends can help clarify particular issues and help you make positive decisions.

"Humanism in a nutshell . . . rejects all forms of supernaturalism, pantheism, and metaphysical idealism, and considers man's supreme ethical aim as working for the welfare of all humanity in this one and only life."

Humanism Promotes Communing with Humanity, Not God

Corliss Lamont

Corliss Lamont (1902–1995) had a wide ranging career as a writer and a social rebel. He fought for civil liberties and promoted social change. In the 1930s he wrote about his travels in the Soviet Union, praising the good qualities of socialism while noting its shortcomings. His book, *The Philosophy of Humanism*, expresses his movement toward humanism later in life. He was made honorary president of the American Humanist Association. In the following viewpoint, Lamont explains the basic beliefs shared by most humanists. Lamont does not view humanism as a religion, but he admits that some humanists view their philosophy as alternative religion.

As you read, consider the following questions:

1. What relative importance does Lamont give to human reason, science, emotions, love, and compassion?
2. Some people believe that we must choose either helping ourselves or helping others. What does Lamont say about this choice?

Adapted from "Naturalistic Humanism," by Corliss Lamont, *The Humanist*, September/October 1971, pp. 9–10, by permission of the Estate of Corliss Lamont.

Humanism is such a warm and attractive word that in the 20th century it has been adopted by various groups, often diametrically opposed in ideology, whose use of it is most questionable. Even the Catholics, who still adhere to every outworn myth of Christian supernaturalism, promote what they call *Catholic Humanism*; while the Marxists, who reject in practice political democracy and civil liberties, continually talk of *Socialist Humanism*.

But the Humanism that has become increasingly influential in this century, in English-speaking countries and throughout the non-Communist world, is *naturalistic Humanism*. This is the Humanism that I have supported through the written and spoken word for some 50 years.

To define naturalistic Humanism in a nutshell, it rejects all forms of supernaturalism, pantheism, and metaphysical idealism, and considers man's supreme ethical aim as working for the welfare of all humanity in this one and only life, using the methods of reason, science, and democracy for the solution of problems.

To become more specific, Humanism believes, **first,** that Nature or the universe makes up the totality of existence and is completely self-operating according to natural law, with no need for a God or gods to keep it functioning. This cosmos, unbounded in space and infinite in time, consists fundamentally of a constantly changing system of matter and energy, and is neutral in regard to man's well-being and values.

Second, Humanism holds that the race of man is the present culmination of a time-defying evolutionary process on this planet that has lasted billions of years; that each human being exists as an inseparable unity of mind and body, and that therefore after death there can be no personal immortality or survival of consciousness.

Third, in working out its basic views on man and the universe, Humanism relies on reason, and especially on the established facts, laws, and methods of modern experimental science. In general, people's best hope for solving their problems is through the use of intelligence and scientific method applied with vision and determination. Such qualities as courage, love, and perseverance provide emotional drive for successfully coping with difficulties, but it is reason that finds the actual solution.

Fourth, Humanism is opposed to all theories of universal determinism, fatalism, or predestination and believes that human beings possess genuine freedom of choice (free will) in making decisions both important and unimportant. Free choice is conditioned by inheritance, education, the external environment (including economic conditions), and other factors. Nonetheless, it remains real and substantial. Humanism rejects both Marxist economic determinism and Christian theistic determinism.

Fifth, Humanism advocates an ethics or morality that grounds all human values in this-earthly experiences and relationships, and that views man as a functioning unity of physical, emotional, and intellectual faculties. The Humanist holds as his highest ethical goal the this-worldly happiness, freedom, and progress—economic, cultural, and material— of all mankind, irrespective of nation, race, religion, sex, or economic status. Reserving the word *love* for their families and friends, he has an attitude of *compassionate concern* toward his fellow men in general.

The Task of Humanity

Man is at last becoming aware that he alone is responsible for the realization of the world of his dreams, that he has within himself the power for its achievement. He must set intelligence and will to the task.

Paul Kurtz, *Humanist Manifesto I*, 1933.

Sixth, in the controversial realm of sex relations, Humanism rejects entirely dualistic theories that separate soul from body and claim that the highest morality is to keep the soul pure and undefiled from physical pleasure and desire. The Humanist regards sexual emotions and their fulfillment as healthy, beautiful, and Nature's wonderful way of making possible the continued reproduction of the human race. While Humanism advocates high standards of conduct between the sexes, it rejects the puritanism of the past and looks upon sex love and sex pleasure as among the greatest of human experiences and values.

Seventh, Humanism believes that every individual must exercise a considerable amount of self-interest, if only to keep alive and healthy, but that altruistic endeavors on behalf of the community can be harmoniously combined with normal self-interest. Thus the good life is best attained by uniting the more personal satisfactions with important work and other activities that contribute to the welfare of one's city, nation, or other social unit. Significant work usually deepens a person's happiness.

Eighth, Humanism supports the widest possible development of the arts and the awareness of beauty, so that the aesthetic experience may become a pervasive reality in people's lives. The Humanist eschews the artificial distinction between the fine arts and the useful arts and asserts that the common objects of daily use should embody a fusion of utility and grace. The mass production of industrial goods by machinery need not necessarily defeat this aim. Among other things, Humanism calls for the planned architectural reconstruction of towns and cities throughout America, so that beauty may prevail in our urban life.

Ninth, Humanism gives special emphasis to appreciation of the beauty and splendor of Nature. There is no heavenly Father in or behind Nature, but Nature is truly our fatherland. The Humanists energetically back the widespread efforts for conservation, the protection of wild life, and the campaigns to maintain and extend ecological values. Their keen responsiveness to every sort of natural beauty evokes in them a feeling of profound kinship with Nature and its myriad forms of life.

Tenth, for the actualization of human happiness and freedom everywhere on earth, Humanism advocates the establishment of international peace, democracy, and a high standard of living throughout the world. Humanists, in their concern for the welfare of all nations, peoples, and races, adopt William Lloyd Garrison's aphorism, "Our country is the world; our countrymen are all mankind." It follows that Humanists are strongly opposed to all forms of nationalist and racial prejudice.

Eleventh, Humanism believes that the best type of government is some form of political democracy, including civil liberties and full freedom of expression throughout all areas of economic, political, and cultural life. Reason and science are crippled unless they remain unfettered in the pursuit of truth. In the United States, the Humanist militantly supports the fundamental guarantees in the Bill of Rights.

The Goals and Methods of Humanism

We are committed to extending the ideals of reason, freedom, individual and collective opportunity, and democracy throughout the world community. The problems that humankind will face in the future, as in the past, will no doubt be complex and difficult. However, if it is to prevail, it can only do so by enlisting resourcefulness and courage. Secular humanism places trust in human intelligence rather than in divine guidance. Skeptical of theories of redemption, damnation, and reincarnation, secular humanists attempt to approach the human situation in realistic terms: human beings are responsible for their own destinies.

Paul Kurtz, *A Secular Humanist Declaration*, 1980.

Twelfth, Humanism, in accordance with scientific method, encourages the unending questioning of basic assumptions and convictions in every field of thought. This includes, of course, philosophy, naturalistic Humanism, and the 12 points I have outlined in this attempt at definition. Humanism is not a new dogma, but is a developing philosophy ever open to experimental testing, newly discovered facts, and more rigorous reasoning.

I do not claim that every Humanist will accept all of the 12 points I have suggested. There will be particular disagreement, I imagine, on the fourth point; that is, the one concerning free choice.

Not every Humanist wants to use the phrase *naturalistic* Humanism. Some prefer the term *scientific* Humanism, *secular* Humanism, or *democratic* Humanism. There is also a large group who consider Humanism a *religion* and who find an institutional home in the Fellowship of Religious Humanists, with its quarterly journal, *Religious Humanism*. For my own part, I prefer to call naturalistic Humanism a philosophy or way of life.

CHAPTER 4

How Should We Make Moral Decisions?

Chapter Preface

While some people are content to discuss theological and philosophical questions for long periods of time, others impatiently demand a practical discussion of the immediate moral dilemmas of their everyday lives. This demand for simple, "to the point" answers can be seen in the work of Robert Ringer. In his viewpoint, Ringer states that it is possible to find "a simple, uncomplicated life" by simply "looking out for number one." Ringer explains that we need to reject all traditional values and morals which others impose on us. We should rationally seek our own happiness. He has confidence that if everyone followed his simple formula for life, we would find social harmony as well as personal pleasure.

In contrast to Ringer's approach to morality, Paul Brownback writes that we should avoid focusing on ourselves. Brownback warns us to neither love ourselves nor hate ourselves. Brownback, writing from the context of Christianity, explains that we should forget ourselves. Rather than focusing on ourselves in either positive or negative ways, we should escape ourselves. Our lives and decisions should be directed toward serving God and others.

Joseph Fletcher offers yet another perspective. He writes that we should not wrap our lives around long lists of rules. Like Ringer, Fletcher rejects the idea that rules should dominate our lives and recommends that the decision-making process be made simple. However, Fletcher rejects Ringer's emphasis on personal, private happiness. Fletcher explains that our decisions should be guided by love for others. Fletcher explains that if we carefully and rationally seek ways to love others, we will always make the right decision.

C.S. Lewis agrees that people should not focus their lives on obeying long lists of rules. Lewis tells his readers that it is not enough to merely submit various areas of our lives to obeying God's commands. Lewis explains that true Christianity demands that the individual give his or her whole life to God. According to Lewis, this total submission to God will make the individual into the kind of person he or she was meant to be. As a result of such submission, the individual will act in moral ways because he or she has become a moral person.

In contrast to those who would base morality on a conscious adherence to a greater purpose or higher reality, James Q. Wilson and Frank R. Zindler write that morality is based on biological evolution. Wilson's goal is to show that morality is neither subject to the individual's taste, nor culturally relative. Wilson believes that humans instinctively have a sense of right and wrong. Thus, Wilson claims that morals are true for all people. Zindler explains that humans have developed certain traits over millions of years (such as sympathy, long-term commitments, self sacrifice, and rational planning). Zindler points out that our moral traits have nothing to do with religious beliefs. He concludes that we need to understand the evolutionary roots of our morality and follow our instinctive urges toward love, beauty, and creativity.

Fred E. Katz does not explain whether religion or biology should guide our decisions. Rather he gives us a general warning about how we make our choices. Katz begins his warning by reminding us of the Holocaust and other tragic events where millions of innocent people were slaughtered in the twentieth century. Then, he reminds us that the Holocaust and other such events were made possible by thousands of ordinary soldiers and citizens who were simply following their "career paths." Katz warns that "minding our own business" in our careers and social lives can cause great evil. Katz thus stands in stark contrast to Robert Ringer, the first author in this chapter.

> "*Looking out for Number One is important because it leads to a simple, uncomplicated life in which you spend more time doing those things which give you the greatest amount of pleasure.*"

Look Out for Number One

Robert Ringer

Robert Ringer has written a series of books promoting his philosophy of "looking out for number one." He has published *Winning Through Intimidation* (1973), *Looking Out For Number One* (1977), *Million Dollar Habits* (1990), and *Getting What You Want: Seven Principles of Rational Living* (2000). Ringer explains in this viewpoint that all humans have a common goal in life: pleasure. Ringer hopes to simplify people's lives by helping them seek rational ways to reach that goal.

As you read, consider the following questions:
1. What does the author mean when he uses the term "looking out for number one"?
2. Imagine a situation in which a person's happiness harmed other people, but those people were too weak to cause the first person any pain. Should the first person go ahead and seek their own happiness? What would Ringer say? What do you believe?
3. Ringer warns his readers: Do not let others push their values on you. After examining Ringer's use of language and his treatment of his opponents, do you think he is guilty of pushing his values on others? If so, explain his guilt. If not, explain his innocence.

Excerpts from pp. ix, x, 2, 4, 9, 10, 11, 12, of *Looking Out for Number One*, by Robert Ringer. Copyright © 1977 by Robert J. Ringer. Reprinted by permission of HarperCollins Publishers, Inc.

B efore moving forward, it will be extremely helpful to you to attempt to clear your mind of all preconceived ideas, whether they concern friendship, love, business or any other aspect of life. I realize this is easier said than done, but do try to make the effort; it will be worth your while. . . .

Clear your mind, then. Forget foundationless traditions, forget the "moral" standards others may have tried to cram down your throat, forget the beliefs people may have tried to intimidate you into accepting as "right." Allow your intellect to take control as you read, and, most important, think of yourself—Number One—as a unique individual. . . .

What Is It?

Looking out for Number One is the conscious, rational effort to spend as much time as possible doing those things which bring you the greatest amount of pleasure and less time on those which cause pain. Everyone automatically makes the effort to be happy, so the key word is "rational". . . .

Because people always do that which they *think* will bring them the greatest pleasure, selfishness is not the issue. Therefore, when people engage in what appear to be altruistic acts, they are not being selfless, as they might like to believe (and might like to have you believe). What they are doing is acting with a lack of awareness. Either they are not completely aware of what they're doing, or they are not aware of why they're doing it, or both. In any case, they are acting selfishly—but not rationally. . . .

What's the Payoff?

Why is it important to act out of choice? What's in it for you? You already know: more pleasure and less pain—a better life for Number One.

In everyday terms, it means feeling refreshed instead of tired. It means making enough money to be able comfortably to afford the material things you want out of life instead of being bitter about not having them. It means enjoying love relationships instead of longing for them. It means experiencing warm friendships instead of concentrating your thoughts on people for whom you harbor negative feelings. It means feeling healthy instead of lousy. It means having a relatively clear mind instead of one that is cluttered and confused. It means more free time instead of never enough time.

Looking out for Number One is important because it leads to a simple, uncomplicated life in which you spend more time doing those things which give you the greatest amount of pleasure. . . .

When you experience pleasure or an absence of pain, you know one thing: you're *feelin' good.*

When you boil it all down, I think that's what everyone's main objective in life really is—to feel good. Happiness isn't a mysterious condition that needs to be dissected carefully by wordologists or psychologists. It's your state of mind when you're experiencing something pleasurable; it's when you feel good.

Loving Yourself

Your self-concern is for the end of protecting and fostering your abilities, that you may continue to grow. Believing that what is best for you is, ultimately, best for the other person also. You allow yourself time to think, to decide, to develop. You seek the larger ends and the broader services, and from a respect for your own nature, you protect yourself against others. You love your neighbor as yourself, remembering that Jesus thus advocates self-love in no uncertain terms.

David Seabury, *The Art of Selfishness*, 1937.

We sometimes lose sight of the fact that our primary objective is really to be as happy as possible and that all our other objectives, great and small, are only a means to that end. . . .

Is looking out for Number One "right?" As a preface, I find it necessary to describe an old nemesis of mine—a creature who's been running around loose on Planet Earth over the millennia, steadily increasing in number. He is the Absolute Moralist. His mission in life is to whip you and me into line. Like Satan, he disguises himself in various human forms. He may appear as a politician on one occasion, next as a minister, and still later as your mother-in-law.

Whatever his disguise, he is relentless. He'll stalk you to your grave if you let him. If he senses that you're one of his prey—that you do not base your actions on rational self-choice—he'll punish you unmercifully. He will make guilt your bedfellow until you're convinced you're a bad guy.

The Absolute Moralist is the creature—looking deceptively like any ordinary human being—who spends his life deciding what is right for *you*. If he gives to charity, he'll try to shame you into "understanding" that it's your moral duty to give to charity too (usually the charity of his choice). If he believes in Christ, he's certain that it's his moral duty to help you "see the light." (In the most extreme cases, he may even feel morally obliged to kill you in order to "save" you from your disbelief.) If he doesn't smoke or drink, it takes little effort for him "logically" to conclude that smoking and drinking are wrong for you. In essence, all he wants is to run your life. There is only one thing which can frustrate him into leaving you alone, and that is your firm decision never to allow him to impose his beliefs on you.

Eliminate Moral Opinions of Others

In deciding whether it's right to look out for Number One, I suggest that the first thing you do is eliminate from consideration all unsolicited moral opinions of others. Morality—the quality of character—is a very personal and private matter. No other living person has the right to decide what is moral (right or wrong) for you. I further suggest that you make a prompt and thorough effort to eliminate from your life all individuals who claim—by words or actions, directly or by inference—to possess such a right. You should concern yourself only with whether looking out for Number One is moral from your own rational, aware viewpoint.

Looking out for Number One means spending more time doing those things which give you pleasure. It does not, however, give you carte blanche to do whatever you please. It is not hedonistic in concept, because the looking-out-for-Number-One philosophy does not end with the hedonistic assertion that man's primary moral duty lies in the pursuit of pleasure.

Looking out for Number One adds a rational, civilized tag: man's primary moral duty lies in the pursuit of pleasure *so long as he does not forcibly interfere with the rights of others*. . . .

There is a rational reason why forcible interference with others has no place in the philosophy of looking out for

Number One. It's simply not in your best interest. In the long run it will bring you more pain than pleasure—the exact opposite of what you wish to accomplish. It's possible that you may, on occasion, experience short-term pleasure by violating the rights of others, but I assure you that the long-term losses (i.e., pain) from such actions will more than offset any short-term enjoyment. . . .

With absolute morality and hedonism out of the way, I perhaps can best answer the question *Is it right?* by asking you one: Can you see any rational reason why you *shouldn't* try to make your life more pleasurable and less painful, so long as you do not forcibly interfere with the rights of others?

It Is Virtuous to Love Yourself

If it is a virtue to love my neighbor as a human being, it must be a virtue—and not a vice—to love myself, since I am a human being too. . . .

The love for my own self is inseparably connected with the love for any other being.

From this it follows that my own self must be as much an object of my love as another person. *The affirmation of one's own life, happiness, growth, freedom is rooted in one's capacity to love,* i.e., in care, respect, responsibility, and knowledge. If an individual is able to love productively, he loves himself too; if he can love *only* others, he cannot love at all.

Eric Fromm, *The Art of Loving*, 1956.

You have but one life to live. Is there anything unreasonable about watching over that life carefully and doing everything within your power to make it a pleasant and fulfilling one? Is it wrong to be aware of what you're doing and why you're doing it? Is it evil to act out of free choice rather than out of the choice of others or out of blind chance?

Remember, selfishness is not the issue. So-called self-sacrifice is just an irrationally selfish act (doing what you think will make you feel good) committed under the influence of a low awareness level. The truth is that it won't make you feel good—certainly not in the long run, after bitterness over what you've "sacrificed" has had a chance to fester within you. At its extreme, this bitterness eventually can develop into a serious case of absolute moralitis. A person's irrational decision to be self-sacrificial can lead to a bitterness so great that it can be soothed only by his preaching to others the virtue of committing the same error.

You may mean well, but don't try so hard to sacrifice for others. It's unfair to them and a disaster for you. The sad irony is that if you persist in swimming in the dangerous and uncivilized waters of self-sacrifice, those for whom you "sacrifice" often will be worse off for your efforts. If instead you spend your time looking out for Number One, those people for whom you care most will benefit by your actions. It's only when you try to pervert the laws of Nature and make the other person's happiness your first responsibility, relegating yourself to the Number Two position, that you run into trouble. It has never worked, and it will not work for you. It's a law of Nature. The idea that self-sacrifice is virtuous is a law of man. If you're going to expend your energies fighting laws, fight man-made laws; they are worth resisting. The laws of Nature will not budge an inch no matter how great your efforts.

That looking out for Number One brings happiness to others, in addition to Number One, is one of the beautiful realities of life. At best, it benefits you and one or more other persons. At worst, it benefits only you and interferes with no one else. Even in the latter case, it actually is a benefit to others because the happy individual is one more person on this earth who does not represent a potential burden to the rest of the population.

That, in my opinion, is enough to make it right. If you practice the principles of looking out for Number One, you'll find it easier to develop rewarding relationships with other human beings, both friends and lovers. It will enhance your ability to be a warm and sensitive person and to enjoy all that life has to offer.

> "*Excessive self-love may be as bad or worse than low self-esteem, but the symptoms are more compatible with our society and so are not as evident because of the value system we have adopted.*"

It Is Dangerous to Love Ourselves

Paul Brownback

Paul Brownback's education includes a B.S. from the United States Military Academy at West Point, a degree in theology from Talbot School of Theology in California, and a Ph.D. from New York University. He was president of Citadel Bible College in Arkansas when he wrote this selection regarding "self-love." Brownback seeks to find a third alternative between two extreme ways of viewing ourselves. He rejects the negative, low self-esteem which troubles many people. But he also rejects the popular solution of telling people to have high self-esteem and pride. Writing from a Christian perspective, he suggests that people should "forget" themselves and focus on other people and on God.

As you read, consider the following questions:

1. According to Brownback, what is wrong with the extremes of self-love and self-hatred?
2. Brownback gives two examples of people "forgetting" themselves. Can you think of other examples which might support Brownback's argument? Can you think of examples which would not support the author's argument?

Excerpted from Paul Brownback, *The Danger of Self-Love* (Chicago: Moody Press, 1982). Copyright © 1982 by The Moody Bible Institute of Chicago. Reprinted with permission.

W e need to recognize that at least on one point self-[love] theory has laid a valid emphasis. From a biblical perspective we cannot imagine that God has planned a life of self-castigation for us. A "Woe is me" attitude hardly need characterize our daily lives.

We could conclude the same from a human standpoint as well. A person who lives in constant awareness of failure and guilt probably is not going to be an effective spouse, parent, neighbor, or a fruitful Christian.

Self-Love vs. Self-Hatred

Because a deep awareness of low self-esteem is so devastating we can understand why many people in that situation have looked to self-love as a welcome alternative. And from a human point of view, it is; a person with high self-esteem can fight his way through life more successfully and with less trauma then one with low self-esteem. Given that fact, it is little wonder that self-theory has become so popular in secular and Christian circles. It also is not surprising that converts in both camps say, "I know it works. It has helped me." No doubt it has, in the sense that the old problems of inferiority, fearfulness, and being dominated are gone, or at least are not as acute.

The question is, though, whether that is God's way of getting through life. Is that His answer to low self-esteem? It is doubtful whether we have solved the problem or merely exchanged symptoms. In medicine some "cures" produce side effects almost as detrimental as the disease itself. Excessive self-love may be as bad or worse than low self-esteem, but the symptoms are more compatible with our society and so are not as evident because of the value system we have adopted.

We have suggested that 2 Timothy 3:1–5 is in fact a list of some by-products of self-love. From a biblical standpoint those things are a cause for alarm, but we must realize that they probably are not considered to be all that bad by our society. Many are accepted and even embraced.

Perhaps one of the reasons the Bible has so much to say about pride and so little to say about low self-esteem is that the person suffering from the latter feels the pain and is aware of his need for help, whereas the person living in pride is in a far more comfortable position. The proud assert themselves, dominate others, get what they want (at the expense of others if necessary), and then others exalt them out of fear and respect for their wealth and power.

So we admit that the proud person, the one with high self-esteem, does do better in this life, but he does so by using a method that is neither taught nor blessed by the Scriptures. However, we have concluded as well that a life of low self-esteem cannot be the answer. What then is that third alternative?

An Alternative to Self-Love

Perhaps a couple of opening illustrations will help us focus our thinking on this new topic. I shall never forget New Year's Day, 1978. The University of Arkansas Razorbacks had won a bid to the Orange Bowl football classic. To add to the excitement, the opponent was Oklahoma, an old and bitter rival. As if that was not enough, before the game several key Arkansas players were booted off the team for misconduct. A furor erupted, but the decision held firm. What started out as a great rivalry now became a "holy war" to determine whether it really did pay to do the right thing.

From the first snap of the ball Arkansas went on a tear, moving up and down the field almost at will. In the midst of all the excitement my sophisticated wife momentarily set aside her genteel Pennsylvania upbringing and began yelling instructions to the coach, players, and occasionally, to the referee. As I look back on the occasion perhaps the best way to describe her reaction is to say that she "forgot herself" completely.

It has always amazed me in my years of teaching homiletics [public speaking] that the straight-faced, dead-pan, rigid student putting everyone to sleep in the classroom is the same young man who the night before in the dormitory, with a ring of friends around him, was expounding in great homiletic form. What made the difference? In the classroom he was "self-conscious," but in the dorm he "forgot himself."

Now I am not talking about a person throwing out all restraint and allowing his instincts to drive him where they will. I am referring to the focus of the mind. My wife was absorbed totally in the game. The student in the dorm was concentrating on his message to his friends. But what happened in the classroom? With all eyes focused on him, he began to ask himself some questions. "How do I look?" "Do they like me?" "Will I remember what comes next?" "How are my gestures?" He became what we call self-conscious.

Self: Paradise or Problem

It should be obvious . . . that the relentless and single-minded search for and glorification of the self is at direct cross-purposes with the Christian injunction to *lose* the self. Certainly Jesus Christ neither lived nor advocated a life that would qualify by today's standards as "self-actualized." For the Christian the self is the problem, not the potential paradise. Understanding this problem involves an awareness of sin, especially of the sin of pride; correcting this condition requires the practice of such un-self-actualized states as contrition and penitence, humility, obedience, and trust in God.

Paul C. Vitz, *Psychology As Religion*, 1977.

The point is that it is possible for a person to "lose himself" in what he is doing. Is that good or bad? In the student's case it was good, because as he lost his self-concern his personality and natural vibrancy surfaced.

Going Beyond "Self"

The situations described above illustrate in a limited way the alternative to self-love we are suggesting. We believe the biblical alternative to the wave of concern over self-image is have *no self-image at all*. Underlying that approach is the fact that both self-love and self-hate are self-centered attitudes. As we shall see, that inward focus is destructive in nature, whereas a focus on others is productive. By changing the direction of our emotional occupation from inward to outward we alleviate the destructive results of self-centered emotions and realize the blessings of a preoccupation with others.

Now if this kind of experience that happens to all of us on occasion was to become the *pattern* of one's life; if his involvement with and concern for others was so intense that he "forgot himself"; if even his daily work was done so wholeheartedly that he was not aware of himself; if when the work was finished he became "lost" in communion with the Lord; *then* he could cease worrying about his self-image. In effect he would have none! The goal is to focus on others, and the negative qualities of both low and high self-esteem will disappear.

But it is fair to ask if such a goal can be achieved. Is it unrealistic even to suggest it? We think not, because as we shall see the Bible calls us to an other-oriented way of living, a life whose total focus is the Lord, others, and that which the Lord has called us to do.

To help clarify what we mean here we should specify what we do *not* mean by other-oriented living, or excluding self-image from our awareness. First, we are not advocating the elimination of all self-evaluation. That is a vital aspect of life. In Romans 12:3, a much misunderstood verse, Paul calls us to evaluate our capacities for service (not to feel good about ourselves). We *need* to evaluate our performance for the purpose of managing our lives effectively for the Lord.

But as William James pointed out, there is an important distinction between that type of evaluation and self-feelings or self-esteem. Self-evaluation is more of an objective process whereas self-esteem is almost exclusively subjective. The former looks at our level of competency in a given area or how well we have performed a given task. The latter has to do with our worth or status. James said those were distinct categories and not necessarily related.

In addition when we speak of other-oriented living we are not talking about the elimination of self-image altogether but the elimination of self-image *from our awareness.* For example, let us assume that when he thinks about himself a person has a tendency toward negative self-feelings. We are not necessarily talking about either trying to deny or change that tendency. Rather, our goal is an outward focus so that the negative tendency is not activated habitually.

> *"Situation ethics . . . calls upon us to keep law in a subservient place, so that only love and reason really count when the chips are down!"*

Love Others and Stay Flexible

Joseph Fletcher

Joseph Fletcher (1905–1991) grew up surrounded by the injustices experienced by poor coal workers in West Virginia. His long, active life included: working in coal mines, receiving a degree in theology from Berkeley Divinity School, studying economics at Yale, serving as a union organizer, teaching ethics and theology at various universities, and pioneering the field of medical ethics. When in college, Fletcher embraced Christianity as a way to improve society. Later in his life he rejected Christianity. The single thread running through his multifaceted life was his activism against injustice. Fletcher was most well-known for his approach to ethics, known as situation ethics. In this viewpoint he compares his ethical thoughts to legalism (fixed moral rules) and antinomianism (the denial of all moral rules), two approaches to ethics with which he strongly disagrees.

As you read, consider the following questions:
1. Why does Fletcher reject legalism and antinomianism?
2. What does the author mean when he writes, "make full and respectful use of principles, . . . treated as maxims but not as laws"?
3. The idea of "love" is very important to Fletcher's thoughts. How would you define his use of this term?

Reproduced from *Situation Ethics: The New Morality*, by Joseph Fletcher. Used by permission of Westminster John Knox Press.

There are at bottom only three alternative routes or approaches to follow in making moral decisions. They are: (1) the legalistic; (2) the antinomian, the opposite extreme—i.e., a lawless or unprincipled approach; and (3) the situational. All three have played their part in the history of Western morals, legalism being by far the most common and persistent. Just as legalism triumphed among the Jews after the exile, so, in spite of Jesus' and Paul's revolt against it, it has managed to dominate Christianity constantly from very early days. . . .

Three Approaches to Decision-Making
1. Legalism

With this approach one enters into every decision-making situation encumbered with a whole apparatus of prefabricated rules and regulations. Not just the spirit but the letter of the law reigns. Its principles, codified in rules, are not merely guidelines or maxims to illuminate the situation; they are *directives* to be followed. Solutions are preset, and you can "look them up" in a book—a Bible or a confessor's manual.

Judaism, Catholicism, Protestantism—all major Western religious traditions have been legalistic. In morals as in doctrine they have kept to a spelled-out, "systematic" orthodoxy. The ancient Jews, especially under the post-exilic Maccabean and Pharisaic leadership, lived by the law or Torah, and its oral tradition (halakah). It was a code of 613 (or 621) precepts, amplified by an increasingly complicated mass of Mishnaic interpretations and applications.

Statutory and code law inevitably piles up, ruling upon ruling, because the complications of life and the claims of mercy and compassion combine—even with code legalists—to accumulate an elaborate system of exceptions and compromise, in the form of rules for breaking the rules! . . .

2. Antinomianism

Over against legalism, as a sort of polar opposite, we can put antinomianism. This is the approach with which one enters into the decision-making situation armed with no principles or maxims whatsoever, to say nothing of *rules*. In every "existential moment" or "unique" situation, it declares, one must rely upon the situation of itself, *there and then*, to provide its ethical solution. . . .

While legalists are preoccupied with law and its stipulations, the Gnostics [a type of antinomianism] are so flatly opposed to law—even in principle—that their moral decisions are random, unpredictable, erratic, quite anomalous. Making moral decisions is a matter of spontaneity; it is literally unprincipled, purely *ad hoc* and casual. They follow no forecastable course from one situation to another. They are, exactly, anarchic—i.e., without a rule. They are not only "unbound by the chains of law" but actually sheer extemporizers, impromptu and intellectually irresponsible. They not only cast the old Torah [Jewish Law] aside; they even cease to think seriously and *care-fully* about the demands of love as it has been shown in Christ, the love norm itself. . . .

3. Situationism

A third approach, in between legalism and antinomian unprincipledness, is situation ethics. (To jump from one polarity to the other would be only to go from the frying pan to the fire.) The situationist enters into every decision-making situation fully armed with the ethical maxims of his community and its heritage, and he treats them with respect as illuminators of his problems. Just the same he is prepared in any situation to compromise them or set them aside *in the situation* if love seems better served by doing so.

Situation ethics goes part of the way with natural law, by accepting reason as the instrument of moral judgment, while rejecting the notion that the good is "given" in the nature of things, objectively. It goes part of the way with Scriptural law by accepting revelation as the source of the norm while rejecting all "revealed" norms or laws but the one command—to love God in the neighbor. The situationist follows a moral law or violates it according to love's need.

In non-Christian situation ethics some other highest good or *summum bonum* will, of course, take love's place as the one and only standard—such as self-realization in the ethics of Aristotle. But the *Christian* is neighbor-centered first and last. Love is for people, not for principles; i.e., it is personal—and therefore when the impersonal universal conflicts with the personal particular, the latter prevails in situation ethics. Because of its mediating position, prepared to act on moral laws or in spite of them, the antinomians will call situationists soft legalists, and legalists will call them cryptoantinomians.

Principles, Yes, but Not Rules

It is necessary to insist that situation ethics is willing to make full and respectful use of principles, to be treated as maxims but not as laws or precepts. We might call it "principled relativism." To repeat the term used above, principles or maxims or general rules are *illuminators*. But they are not *directors*. The classic rule of moral theology has been to follow laws but do it *as much as possible* according to love and according to reason. Situation ethics, on the other hand, calls upon us to keep law in a subservient place, so that *only* love and reason really count when the chips are down! . . .

Morality Is Humanistic Not Theistic

For the past thirty years I have seen a lot of what goes on in the secular professions, the "helping professions" of social workers, people in public services, and physicians, and I have always been impressed by how nonreligious their decision-making is and how consistently they ignore and bypass religious beliefs and theological doctrines. They consistently and for the most part constructively disregard "commandment ethics" and choose instead whatever courses of action rationally promise the most humanly beneficial consequences. It is human benefit, not "revealed" or "divine" norms, that provides the moral values of serious decision-makers. In other words, their morality is humanistic, not theistic.

Joseph Fletcher, *Free Inquiry*, 1987.

Nevertheless, in situation ethics even the most revered principles may be thrown aside if they conflict in any concrete case with love. Even Karl Barth, who writes vehemently of "absolutely wrong" actions, allows for what he calls the *ultima ratio*, the outside chance that love in a particular situation might override the absolute. The instance he gives is abortion.

Using terms made popular by Tillich and others, we may

say that Christian situationism is a method that proceeds, so to speak, from (1) its one and only law, *agape* (love), to (2) the *sophia* (wisdom) of the church and culture, containing many "general rules" of more or less reliability, to (3) the *kairos* (moment of decision, the fullness of time) in which *the responsible self in the situation* decides whether the *sophia* can serve love there, or not. This is the situational strategy in capsule form. To legalists it will seem to treat the *sophia* without enough reverence and obedience; to antinomians it will appear befuddled and "inhibited" by the *sophia*.

Legalists make an idol of the *sophia*, antinomians repudiate it, situationists *use* it. They cannot give to any principle less than love more than tentative consideration, for they know, with Dietrich Bonhoeffer, "The question of the good is posed and is decided in the midst of each definite, yet unconcluded, unique and transient situation of our lives, in the midst of our living relationships with men, things, institutions and powers, in other words in the midst of our historical existence." And Bonhoeffer, of course, is a modern Christian ethicist who was himself executed for trying to kill, even *murder*, Adolf Hitler—so far did he go as a situationist.

"Christ says 'Give me All. I don't want so much of your time and so much of your money and so much of your work: I want You.'"

Morality Begins with a Commitment to God, Not to Rules

C.S. Lewis

C.S. Lewis (1898–1963) was a literary scholar, who taught at Oxford and Cambridge universities in England. As a young man, Lewis rejected all religion. Later he become convinced of the reality of Christianity. He spent much of his life explaining the truth of Christianity in novels, children's literature, radio programs, and books. In this viewpoint, Lewis discusses how Christianity makes the process of decision making both easier and harder. Lewis writes that a Christian should not focus on obeying this or that rule; rather the person should give himself or herself totally to God.

As you read, consider the following questions:
1. Why does Lewis write that the Christian approach to morality is both easier and harder?
2. Lewis writes that the lazy school boy must ultimately work harder than the diligent student. What does Lewis mean by this illustration?
3. Why does Lewis compare the State to the Church?

Excerpted from *The Joyful Christian* by C.S. Lewis. Copyright © C.S. Lewis Pte. Ltd. 1977. Reprinted by permission.

The ordinary idea which we all have before we become Christians is this. We take as starting point our ordinary self with its various desires and interests. We then admit that something else—call it "morality" or "decent behavior," or "the good of society"—has claims on this self: claims which interfere with its own desires. What we mean by "being good" is giving in to those claims. Some of the things the ordinary self wanted to do turn out to be what we call "wrong": well, we must give them up. Other things, which the self did not want to do, turn out to be what we call "right": well, we shall have to do them. But we are hoping all the time that when all the demands have been met, the poor natural self will still have some chance, and some time, to get on with its own life and do what it likes. In fact, we are very like an honest man paying his taxes. He pays them all right, but he does hope that there will be enough left over for him to live on. Because we are still taking our natural self as the starting point.

As long as we are thinking that way, one or the other of two results is likely to follow. Either we give up trying to be good, or else we become very unhappy indeed. For, make no mistake: if you are really going to try to meet all the demands made on the natural self, it will not have enough left over to live on. The more you obey your conscience, the more your conscience will demand of you. And your natural self, which is thus being starved and hampered and worried at every turn, will get angrier and angrier. In the end, you will either give up trying to be good, or else become one of those people who, as they say, "live for others" but always in a discontented, grumbling way—always wondering why the others do not notice it more and always making a martyr of yourself. And once you have become that, you will be a far greater pest to anyone who has to live with you than you would have been if you had remained frankly selfish.

The Whole Self, Not Part

The Christian way is different: harder, and easier. Christ says "Give me All. I don't want so much of your time and so much of your money and so much of your work: I want You. I have not come to torment your natural self, but to kill it. No half-measures are any good. I don't want to cut off a branch here and a branch there, I want to have the whole tree down. I don't want to drill the tooth, or crown it, or stop it, but to have it out. Hand over the whole natural self, all the desires which you think innocent as well as the ones you think wicked—the whole outfit. I will give you a new self instead. In fact, I will give you Myself: my own will shall become yours."

Both harder and easier than what we are all trying to do. You have noticed, I expect, that Christ Himself sometimes describes the Christian way as very hard, sometimes as very easy. He says, "Take up your Cross"—in other words, it is like going to be beaten to death in a concentration camp. Next minute he says, "My yoke is easy and my burden light." He means both. And one can just see why both are true.

Teachers will tell you that the laziest boy in the class is the one who works hardest in the end. They mean this. If you give two boys, say, a proposition in geometry to do, the one who is prepared to take trouble will try to understand it. The lazy boy will try to learn it by heart because, for the moment, that needs less effort. But six months later, when they are preparing for an exam, that lazy boy is doing hours and hours of miserable drudgery over things the other boy understands, and positively enjoys, in a few minutes. Laziness means more work in the long run. Or look at it this way. In a battle, or in mountain climbing, there is often one thing which it takes a lot of pluck to do; but it is also, in the long run, the safest thing to do. If you funk it, you will find yourself, hours later, in far worse danger. The cowardly thing is also the most dangerous thing.

It is like that here. The terrible thing, the almost impossible thing, is to hand over your whole self—all your wishes and precautions—to Christ. But it is far easier than what we are all trying to do instead. For what we are trying to do is to remain what we call "ourselves," to keep personal happiness as our great aim in life, and yet at the same time be "good." We are all trying to let our mind and heart go their own way—centered on money or pleasure or ambition—and hoping, in spite of this, to behave honestly and chastely and humbly. And that is exactly what Christ warned us you could not do. As He said, a thistle cannot produce figs. If I am a field that contains nothing but grass-seed, I cannot produce wheat. Cutting the grass may keep it short: but I shall still produce grass and no wheat. If I want to produce wheat, the change must go deeper than the surface. I must be ploughed up and resown.

Creating Ourselves in the Context of Morals

People often think of Christian morality as a kind of bargain in which God says, "If you keep a lot of rules, I'll reward you, and if you don't I'll do the other thing." I do not think that is the best way of looking at it. I would much rather say that every time you make a choice you are turning the central part of you, the part of you that chooses, into something a little different from what it was before. And taking your life as a whole, with all your innumerable choices, all your life long you are slowly turning this central thing either into a Heaven creature or into a hellish creature: either into a creature that is in harmony with God, and with other creatures, and with itself, or else into one that is in a state of war and hatred with God, and with its fellow creatures, and with itself. To be the one kind of creature is Heaven: that is, it is joy, and peace, and knowledge, and power. To be the other means madness, horror, idiocy, rage, impotence, and eternal loneliness. Each of us at each moment is progressing to the one state or the other.

C.S. Lewis, in *The Joyful Christian*, 1977.

That is why the real problem of the Christian life comes where people do not usually look for it. It comes the very moment you wake up each morning. All your wishes and hopes for the day rush at you like wild animals. And the first job each morning consists simply in shoving them all back; in listening to that other voice, taking that other point of view, letting that other larger, stronger, quieter life come flowing in. And so on, all day. Standing back from all your natural fussings and frettings; coming in out of the wind.

Becoming a New Person

We can only do it for moments at first. But from those moments the new sort of life will be spreading through our system: because now we are letting Him work at the right part of us. It is the difference between paint, which is merely laid on the surface, and a dye or stain which soaks right through. He never talked vague, idealistic gas. When He said, "Be perfect," He meant it. He meant that we must go in for the full treatment. It is hard; but the sort of compromise we are all hankering after is harder—in fact, it is impossible. It may be hard for an egg to turn into a bird: it would be a jolly sight harder for it to learn to fly while remaining an egg. We are like eggs at present. And you cannot go on indefinitely being just an ordinary, decent egg. We must be hatched or go bad.

May I come back to what I said before? This is the whole of Christianity. There is nothing else. It is so easy to get muddled about that. It is easy to think that the Church has a lot of different objects—education, building, missions, holding services. Just as it is easy to think the State has a lot of different objects—military, political, economic, and what not. But in a way things are much simpler than that. The State exists simply to promote and to protect the ordinary happiness of human beings in this life. A husband and wife chatting over a fire, a couple of friends having a game of darts in a pub, a man reading a book in his own room or digging in his own garden—that is what the State is there for. And unless they are helping to increase and prolong and protect such moments, all the laws, parliaments, armies, courts, police, economics, etc., are simply a waste of time. In the same way the Church exists for nothing else but to draw men into Christ, to make them little Christs. If they are not doing that, all the cathedrals, clergy, missions, sermons, even the Bible itself, are simply a waste of time. God became Man for no other purpose. It is even doubtful, you know, whether the whole universe was created for any other purpose. It says in the Bible that the whole universe was made for Christ and that everything is to be gathered together in Him. . . .

What we have been told is how we men can be drawn into Christ—can become part of that wonderful present which the young Prince of the universe wants to offer to His Father—that present which is Himself and therefore us in Him. It is the only thing we were made for. And there are strange, exciting hints in the Bible that when we are drawn in, a great many other things in Nature will begin to come right. The bad dream will be over: it will be morning.

"*People have a natural moral sense, a sense that is formed out of the interaction of their innate dispositions with their familial experiences.*"

We Have an Innate Sense of Right and Wrong

James Q. Wilson

James Q. Wilson has taught political science at the University of Chicago, Harvard University, and the University of California, Los Angeles. He has written numerous books on police and criminal behavior, politics, and urban issues. In the following viewpoint, Wilson defends the idea that all humans have a "moral sense," an innate awareness of right and wrong. Recognizing the controversial nature of his position, he spends a great deal of time defending the possibility of a moral sense which is somehow rooted in our evolution. Wilson rejects the idea that our ultimate values change from one culture to the next. Rather, he maintains that people need to cultivate the innate sense of right and wrong which we all share.

As you read, consider the following questions:

1. According to Wilson, how have people's assumptions about the "moral sense" (moral instincts) changed in history?
2. What examples are given in this viewpoint to support the idea that all humans have a moral sense?
3. Do you believe that Wilson is correct in assuming that when people give excuses or justify their behavior, it proves that they have an innate sense of morality?

Reprinted and abridged with the permission of The Free Press, a division of Simon & Schuster, Inc., from *The Moral Sense*, by James Q. Wilson. Copyright © 1993 by James Q. Wilson.

Since daily newspapers were first published, they have been filled with accounts of murder and mayhem, of political terror and human atrocities. Differences in religious belief so minor as to be invisible to all but a trained theologian have been the pretext, if not the cause, of unspeakable savageries. Differences in color and even small differences in lineage among people of the same color have precipitated riots, repression, and genocide. The Nazi regime set about to exterminate an entire people and succeeded in murdering six million of them before an invading army put a stop to the methodical horror. Hardly any boundary can be drawn on the earth without it becoming a cause for war. In parts of Africa, warlords fight for power and booty while children starve. When riots occur in an American city, many bystanders rush to take advantage of the opportunity for looting. If people have a common moral sense, there is scarcely any evidence of it in the matters to which journalists—and their readers—pay the greatest attention.

A person who contemplates this endless litany of tragedy and misery would be pardoned for concluding that man is at best a selfish and aggressive animal whose predatory instincts are only partially and occasionally controlled by some combination of powerful institutions and happy accidents. He would agree with the famous observation of Thomas Hobbes that in their natural state men engage in a war of all against all. In this respect they are worse than beasts; whereas the animals of the forest desire only sufficient food and sex, humans seek not merely sufficient but abundant resources. Men strive to outdo one another in every aspect of life, pursuing power and wealth, pride and fame, beyond any reasonable measure.

Being Moral Is Normal

But before drawing so bleak a conclusion from his daily newspaper, the reader should ask himself why bloodletting and savagery are news. There are two answers. The first is that they are unusual. If daily life were simply a war of all against all, what would be newsworthy would be the occasional outbreak of compassion and decency, self-restraint and fair dealing. Our newspapers would mainly report on parents who sacrificed for their children and people who aided neighbors in distress. Amazed that such things occurred, we would explain them as either rare expressions of a personality quirk or disguised examples of clever self-dealing. The second reason that misery is news is because it is shocking. We recoil in horror at pictures of starving children, death camp victims, and greedy looters. Though in the heat of battle or the embrace of ideology many of us will become indifferent to suffering or inured to bloodshed, in our calm and disinterested moments we discover in ourselves an intuitive and powerful aversion to inhumanity.

This intuition is not simply a cultural artifact or a studied hypocrisy. The argument of this book is that people have a natural moral sense, a sense that is formed out of the interaction of their innate dispositions with their earliest familial experiences. To different degrees among different people, but to some important degree in almost all people, that moral sense shapes human behavior and the judgments people make of the behavior of others.

A Recent History of "Morality"

At one time, the view that our sense of morality shaped our behavior and judgments was widely held among philosophers. Aristotle said that man was naturally a social being who seeks happiness. Thomas Aquinas, the great medieval theologian who sought to reconcile Catholic and Aristotelian teachings, argued that man has a natural inclination to be a rational and familial being; the moral law is, in the first instance, an expression of a natural—that is, an innate—tendency. Adam Smith wrote that man is motivated by sympathy as well as by self-interest, and he developed a moral philosophy squarely based on this capacity for sympathy. No one can say what effect these doctrines had on the way people actually lived, but one can say that for much of Western history philosophy sought to support and explicate the more social side of human nature without denying its selfish and wilder side.

Modern philosophy, with some exceptions, represents a fundamental break with that tradition. For the last century or so, few of the great philosophical theories of human behavior have accorded much weight to the possibility that men and women are naturally endowed with anything remotely resembling a moral sense. Marxism as generally received (and, with some exceptions, as Marx himself wrote it) is a relentlessly materialistic doctrine in which morality, religion, and philosophy have no independent meaning; they are, in Marx's words, "phantoms formed in the human brain," "ideological reflexes," "sublimates of their material life-process." . . .

If Marx hinted at morality without examining it, much of modern philosophy abandoned morality without even a hint. Analytical philosophers took seriously the argument that "values" could not be derived from "facts," and tended to relegate moral judgments to the realm of personal preferences not much different from a taste for vanilla ice cream. In 1936 A.J. Ayer asserted that since moral arguments (unlike the theory of gravity) cannot be scientifically verified, they are nothing more than "ejaculations or commands," "pure expressions of feeling" that have "no objective validity whatsoever." Existentialists such as Jean-Paul Sartre argued that man must choose his values, but provided little guidance for making that choice. Of course there are many other, quite different tendencies in modern philosophy, but anyone who has spent much time in a classroom is keenly aware that the skeptical, relativistic themes have been most influential. Richard Rorty, perhaps the most important philosophical writer in present-day America, denies that there is anything like a "core self" or an inherently human quality, and so there is no way for us to say that some actions are inherently inhuman, even when confronted with the horrors of Auschwitz (which, of course, Rorty condemns, but only because history and circumstance have supplied him with certain "beliefs").

What Marxism and positivism have meant for philosophy, Freudianism has meant for psychology. It is difficult to disentangle what Freud actually said from what he is widely believed to have said, or one stage in his thinking from another. But it seems clear that Freudianism was popularly understood as meaning that people have instincts, especially sexual and aggressive ones, and not moral senses; morality, to the extent people acquire any, is chiefly the result of learning to repress those instincts. Among the objects of the sexual drive are one's own parents. Repressing those instincts is necessary for civilization to exist, but that repression can lead to mental illness. People do acquire a conscience—Freud called it the superego—but not out of any natural inclination to be good; rather, their conscience is an internalized fear of losing the love of their parents. Freud, at least, argued that conscience existed; some behavioral psychologists, such as B.F. Skinner, denied even that.

Cultural Relativism

People who have never been affected by Marxism or Freudianism and who are indifferent to philosophical disputes may nonetheless have learned, at least secondhand, the teachings of many cultural anthropologists. All of us are aware of the great variety of social customs, religious beliefs, and ritual practices to be found around the world, especially among primitive peoples, a variety so great as to suggest that all morality is relative to time and place. And if we wish to confirm what our imagination suggests, we can find explicit arguments to that effect in some of the leading texts. In 1906 the great sociologist William Graham Sumner wrote that "the mores can make anything right." Thirty years later Ruth Benedict's best-selling book *Patterns of Culture* was read to mean that all ways of life were equally valid. Published in 1934, just after the Nazis had come to power, it was probably intended to be a plea for tolerance and an argument for judging one's own culture only after becoming aware of an alternative to it. But by popularizing the phrase "cultural relativism" and discussing cannibalism without explicitly condemning it, she was read as saying something like what Sumner had said: culture and the mores of society can make anything right and anything wrong. . . .

If this were true, then my argument that there is in human nature the elements of a natural moral sense would be untrue. There can scarcely be anything worth calling a moral sense if people can be talked out of it by modern philosophy, secular humanism, Marxist dialectics, or pseudo-Freudian psychoanalysis. But I doubt that most people most of the time are affected by these intellectual fashions. The intellectuals who consume them may be affected. If they think life is without moral meaning, they may live accordingly, creating an avant-garde in which "meaning" is to be found in self-expressive art, a bohemian counterculture, or anarchistic politics. But the lives of most people arc centered around the enduring facts of human existence—coping with a family, establishing relationships, and raising children. Everywhere we look, we see ordinary men and women going about their daily affairs, happily or unhappily as their circumstances allow, making and acting on moral judgments without pausing to wonder what Marx or Freud or Rorty would say about those judgments. In the intimate realms of life, there will be stress, deprivation, and frustration, but ordinarily these will not be experienced as a pervasive spiritual crisis. . . .

A Common Moral Sense

Let us suppose that the social bond evolves gradually, growing in power and scope with the size of the human community and the complexity of group life. Clearly it is necessary for each generation to teach its young the rules of social life. But if parents teach moral lessons to their young, we would expect great variation in the lessons taught and learned, as well as many cases in which the parents decided to teach no lessons at all. Moreover, parents will differ in intelligence, temperament, and interests, as will their children. Over the thousands of years during which billions of people have walked their brief moments on this earth, surely we would find many examples of peoples with no social bond at all such that everybody lives only by the rule of personal advantage.* And we should find some societies whose members abandoned their children in wholesale numbers, having decided that nurturing and teaching them was a tiresome burden. But we find neither. . . .

Take murder: in all societies there is a rule that unjustifiable homicide is wrong and deserving of punishment. To justify an exception requires making reasonable arguments. My critics will rejoin that if only *unjustifiable* homicides are wrong, and if societies differ radically in what constitutes a justification, that is tantamount to saying that there is no rule against homicide. I grant the force of their argument, but I suggest in response that the need to make an argument—to offer a justification for the killing—is itself a sign that every society attaches some weight to human life. For murder not to be a universal wrong, one would have to imagine a society in which murder were subject to no general rule other than, perhaps, "only do it when you think you can get away with it."

There is also a rule against incest. Sexual intercourse between brothers and sisters or between mothers and sons is universally condemned. Where lawful exceptions occur, it is because of extraordinary circumstances that are carefully defined—for example, the need to preserve a royal dynasty when suitable mates cannot be found outside the first degree of kinship. For incest not to be a universal wrong, one would have to imagine a society in which sex between brothers and sisters was approved of, or at worst a matter of indifference. So far as anyone is aware, no such society has existed. . . .

Were social norms entirely designed to suit the preferences of people, there would be far fewer children in the world today. Many people would have noticed the great risks, enormous burdens, and uncertain rewards of nurturing babies and decided not to do it. So widespread is the practice of child nurturance and so unreflective is the parental behavior on which it depends that this care must occur, not because a rule is being enforced, but because an impulse is being obeyed. Though a rule may be propounded to control the small fraction of people who prefer to let their offspring die, it is not the rule that explains the behavior of most people but their behavior that explains the rule. For this reason I doubt that the fundamental social bonds are entirely created by human artifice [culture] or preserved by human choice. . . .

If Darwin and his followers are right, and I think they are, the moral sense must have had adaptive value; if it did not, natural selection would have worked against people who had such useless traits as sympathy, self-control, or a desire for fairness and in favor of those with the opposite tendencies (such as a capacity for ruthless predation, or a preference for immediate gratifications, or a disinclination to share). Biologists, beginning with Darwin, have long understood this. But contemporary biologists sometimes give too narrow an account of this evolutionary process. . . .

The Golden Rule

Confucianism
What you don't want done to yourself, don't do to others.
—SIXTH CENTURY, B.C.

Buddhism
Hurt not others with that which pains thyself.
—FIFTH CENTURY, B.C.

Jainism
In happiness and suffering, in joy and grief, we should regard all creatures as we regard our own self, and should therefore refrain from inflicting upon others such injury as would appear undesirable to us if inflicted upon ourselves.
—FIFTH CENTURY, B.C.

Zoroastrianism
Do not do unto others all that which is not well for oneself.
—FIFTH CENTURY, B.C.

Classical Paganism
May I do to others as I would that they should do unto me.
Plato—FOURTH CENTURY, B.C.

Hinduism
Do naught to others which if done to thee would cause thee pain.
Mahabharata—THIRD CENTURY, B.C.

Judaism
What is hateful to yourself, don't do to your fellow man.
Rabbi Hillel—FIRST CENTURY, B.C.

Christianity
Whatsoever ye would that men should do to you, do ye even so to them.
Jesus of Nazareth—FIRST CENTURY, A.D.

Sikhism
Treat others as thou wouldst be treated thyself.
—SIXTEENTH CENTURY, A.D.

This book is a modest effort to supply the evidence that man has a moral sense, one that emerges as naturally as his sense of beauty or ritual (with which morality has much in common) and that will affect his behavior, though not always and in some cases not obviously. The moral "sense" exists in two meanings of the word: First, virtually everyone, beginning at a very young age, makes moral judgments that, though they may vary greatly in complexity, sophistication, and wisdom, distinguish between actions on the grounds that some are right and others wrong, and virtually everyone recognizes that for these distinctions to be persuasive to others they must be, or at least appear to be, disinterested. Second, virtually everyone, beginning at a very young age, acquires a set of social habits that we ordinarily find pleasing in others and satisfying when we practice them ourselves. There are, to be sure, some people who, again from a very young age, seem to have no regular habits that make their company pleasurable to decent people and lack any tendency to judge things as right or wrong in a disinterested way. Such people are rare, as evidenced by the special terms we have for them: the former are wild, the latter psychopathic.

How can one reconcile the existence of a moral sense with the evidence of moral depravity, unmoral oppression, and amoral self-indulgence—that is, with crime, cruelty, and licentious extravagance? There is no puzzle here. The moral sense is no surer a cause of moral action than beliefs are the cause of actions generally. Behavior is the product of our senses interacting with our circumstances. But when we behave in ways that seem to violate our fundamental moral sensibilities—when we abandon children, sacrifice victims, or kill rivals—we offer reasons, and the reasons are never simply that we enjoy such acts and think that we can get away with them. The justifications we supply invariably are based on other claims, higher goods, or deferred pleasures: we need to assure a good crop, reduce suffering, produce a son who can inherit our property, or avert a plague that would devastate the community. Our moral sense requires justification for any departure from it; as circumstances change—as we learn better ways of averting plagues or producing crops—arguments that once seemed adequate begin to seem inadequate, and our behavior changes accordingly. It is this feeling that we must offer justifications for violating a moral standard that explains the difference between a standard that is purely a matter of taste ("I like chocolate ice cream") and one that is a matter of moral sensibility ("I ought not to be cruel"). If we decide to switch to vanilla ice cream, we need not justify our decision, especially by any argument that the new flavor merits our respect; if we are cruel, on the other hand, we feel obliged to justify it, usually by saying that the suffering party deserved his fate.

*Readers familiar with anthropology will claim that such a group has been found. They are the Ik of northern Uganda, described by Colin Turnbull in 1972 as living amid a horrific war of all against all. Children were abandoned, familial affection was nonexistent, and the elderly were encouraged to starve. So dreadful was their behavior that Turnbull urged the government to disperse them forcibly so that their monstrous culture would be destroyed. The Ik family was "not a fundamental unit" (133); the people were "loveless" (234) and engaged in "mutual exploitation (290); coerced relocation was necessary (283). But other scholars have cast serious doubt on the accuracy of Turnbull's account. In 1985 Bernd Heine (who was much more fluent in the Ik language than Turnbull) found them to be a quite sociable people, much different from what Turnbull had described. But scholars seem to remember the Turnbull book and not the Heine refutation (Edgerton, 1992:6–8). A better, though less well known, example of a relatively unsociable people were the Sirioni Indians of eastern Bolivia as described by Allan Holmberg (1950: esp. 77–78). But even here, though the Sirioni often seemed indifferent to the fate of fellow members of the tribe, they loved their own children.

"The principle of 'enlightened self-interest' is an excellent first approximation to an ethical principle which is both consistent with what we know of human nature and is relevant to the problems of life in a complex society."

Religion Is Not Needed in Moral Decisions

Frank R. Zindler

Frank R. Zindler is a retired professor of biology and geology. He is also active in promoting atheism. Zindler writes that religion is not really the foundation of morality, as many people assume. Rather, morality is founded on certain inherited principles as well as our social development. Zindler also challenges his readers to consider how morality needs to evolve beyond the Ten Commandments.

As you read, consider the following questions:
1. If religion is not the foundation of morals, what foundation does Zindler give for ethics?
2. According to the author, how do genetics and the environment influence our moral behavior?
3. What does Zindler mean by "enlightened self-interest"?

Reprinted from "Ethics Without Gods," by Frank R. Zindler, *American Atheist*, February 1985, by permission of the author.

One of the first questions Atheists are asked by true believers and doubters alike is, "If you don't believe in a god, there's nothing to prevent you from committing crimes, is there? Without the fear of hell-fire and eternal damnation, you can do anything you like, can't you?"

It is hard to believe that even intelligent and educated people could hold such an opinion, but they do. It seems never to have occurred to them that the Greeks and Romans, whose gods and goddesses were something less than paragons of virtue, nevertheless led lives not obviously worse than those of the Baptists of Alabama. Moreover, pagans such as Aristotle and Marcus Aurelius—although their systems are not suitable for us today—managed to produce ethical treatises of great sophistication, a sophistication rarely, if ever, equaled by Christian moralists.

The answer to the question posed above is, of course, "Absolutely not!" The behavior of Atheists is subject to the same rules of sociology, psychology, and neurophysiology that govern the behavior of all members of our species, religionists included. Moreover, despite protestations to the contrary, we may assert as a general rule that when religionists practice ethical behavior, it isn't *really* due to their fear of hell-fire and damnation, or to their hopes of heaven. Ethical behavior—regardless of who the practitioner may be—results always from the same causes and is regulated by the same forces, and has nothing to do with the presence or absence of religious belief. The nature of these causes and forces is the subject of this essay.

Psychobiological Foundations

As human beings, we are social animals. Our sociality is the result of evolution, not choice. Natural selection has equipped us with nervous systems which are peculiarly sensitive to the emotional status of our fellows. Among our kind, emotions are contagious, and it is only the rare psychopathic mutants among us who can be happy in the midst of a sad society. It is in our nature to be happy in the midst of happiness, sad in the midst of sadness. It is in our nature, fortunately, to seek happiness for our fellows at the same time as we seek it for ourselves. Our happiness is greater when it is shared.

Nature also has provided us with nervous systems which are, to a considerable degree, imprintable. To be sure, this phenomenon is not as pronounced or as inelectable as it is, say, in geese—where a newly hatched gosling can be "imprinted" to a toy train and will follow it to exhaustion, as if it were its mother. Nevertheless, some degree of imprinting is exhibited by humans. The human nervous system appears to retain its capacity for imprinting well into old age, and it is highly likely that the phenomenon known as "love-at-first-sight" is a form of imprinting. Imprinting is a form of attachment behavior, and it helps us to form strong interpersonal bonds. It is a major force which helps us to break through the ego barrier to create "significant others" whom we can love as much as ourselves. These two characteristics of our nervous system—emotional suggestibility and attachment imprintability—although they are the foundation of all altruistic behavior and art, are thoroughly compatible with the selfishness characteristic of all behaviors created by the process of natural selection. That is to say, to a large extent behaviors which satisfy ourselves will be found, simultaneously, to satisfy our fellows, and *vice-versa*.

This should not surprise us when we consider that among the societies of our nearest primate cousins, the great apes, social behavior is not chaotic, even if gorillas do lack the Ten Commandments! The young chimpanzee does not need an oracle to tell it to honor its mother and to refrain from killing its brothers and sisters. Of course, family squabbles and even murder have been observed in ape societies, but such behaviors are exceptions, not the norm. So too it is in human societies, everywhere and at all times.

The African apes—whose genes are ninety-eight to ninety-nine percent identical to ours—go about their lives as social animals, cooperating in the living of life, entirely without the benefit of clergy and without the commandments of Exodus, Leviticus, or Deuteronomy. It is further cheering to learn that sociobiologists have even observed altruistic behavior among troops of baboons! More than once, in troops attacked by leopards, aged, post-reproduction-age males have been observed to linger at the rear of the escaping troop and to engage the leopard in what often amounts to a suicidal fight. As an old male delays the leopard's pursuit by sacrificing his very life, the females and young escape and live to fulfill their several destinies. The heroism which we see acted out, from time to time, by our fellow men and women, is far older than their religions. Long before the gods were created by the fear-filled minds of our less courageous ancestors, heroism and acts of self-sacrificing love existed. They did not require a supernatural excuse then, nor do they require one now.

Given the general fact, then, that evolution has equipped us with nervous systems biased in favor of social, rather than antisocial, behaviors, is it not true, nevertheless, that antisocial behavior *does* exist? And does it not exist in amounts greater than a reasonable ethicist would find tolerable? Alas, this is true. But is true largely because we live in worlds far more complex than the Paleolithic world in which our nervous systems originated. To understand the ethical significance of this fact, we must digress a bit and review the evolutionary history of human behavior.

Instinctual and Learned Behavior

Today, heredity can control our behavior in only the most general of ways; it cannot dictate precise behaviors appropriate for infinitely varied circumstances. In our world, heredity needs help.

In the world of a fruit fly, by contrast, the problems to be solved are few in number and highly predictable in nature. Consequently, a fruit fly's brain is largely "hard-wired" by heredity. That is to say, most behaviors result from environmental activation of nerve circuits which are formed automatically by the time of emergence of the adult fly. This is an extreme example of what is called instinctual behavior. Each behavior is coded for by a gene or genes which predispose the nervous system to develop certain types of circuits and not others, and it is all but impossible to act contrary to the genetically predetermined script.

The world of a mammal—say a fox—is much more complex and unpredictable than that of the fruit fly. Consequently, a fox is born with only a portion of its neuronal circuitry hard-wired. Many of its neurons remain "plastic" throughout life.

That is, they may or may not hook up with each other in functional circuits, depending upon environmental circumstances. Learned behavior is behavior which results from activation of these environmentally conditioned circuits. Learning allows the individual mammal to assimilate—by trial and error—greater numbers of adaptive behaviors than could be transmitted by heredity. A fox would be wall-to-wall genes if all its behaviors were specified genetically!

Enlightened Self-Interest

In my own life, I've found what moralists and philosophers have called "enlightened self-interest" to be a useful guide in thrashing through some of the more common ethical dilemmas. The phrase "self-interest" has a cold-blooded sound, as if it might lead you to foreclose mortgages on penniless old ladies, but it needn't work that way. Self-interest does not, as some people believe, necessarily imply ruthless manipulation of people or trampling over them and their needs . . . those are unprincipled ways of acting. Just as you can behave barbarously in the service of others (family, country, a "cause"), so, too, can you pursue your own ends in an ethical manner. In fact, if you are self-interested, in the best sense of the phrase, your behavior often falls naturally into conformation with sound, workable ethics. It is people who are confused about their own desires and purposes who generally cause the most havoc, not the self-interested ones.

Phyllis Penn, "Morals, Ethics, and that Cosmo Girl," *Cosmopolitan*, February 1975.

With the evolution of humans, however, environmental complexity increased out of all proportion to the genetic and neuronal changes distinguishing us from our simian ancestors. This was due partly to the fact that our species evolved in a geologic period of great climatic flux—the Ice Ages—and partly to the fact that our behaviors themselves began to change our environment. The changed environment in turn created new problems to be solved. Their solutions further changed the environment, and so on. Thus, the discovery of fire led to the burning of trees and forests, which led to destruction of local water supplies and watersheds, which led to the development of architecture with which to build aqueducts, which led to laws concerning water rights, which led to international strife, and on and on.

Given such complexity, even the ability to learn new behaviors is, by itself, inadequate. If trial and error were the only means, most people would die of old age before they would succeed in rediscovering fire or reinventing the wheel. As a substitute for instinct and to increase the efficiency of learning, mankind developed culture. The ability to teach—as well as to learn—evolved, and trial-and-error learning became a method of last resort.

By transmission of culture—passing on the sum total of the learned behaviors common to a population—we can do what Darwinian genetic selection would not allow: we can inherit acquired characteristics. The wheel once having been invented, its manufacture and use can be passed down through generations. Culture can adapt to change much faster than genes can, and this provides for finely tuned responses to environmental disturbances and upheavals. By means of cultural transmission, those behaviors which have proven useful in the past can be taught quickly to the young, so that adaptation to life—say on the Greenland ice cap—can be assured.

Even so, cultural transmission tends to be rigid: it took over one hundred thousand years to advance to chipping *both* sides of the hand ax! Cultural mutations, like genetic mutations, tend more often than not to be harmful, and both are resisted—the former by cultural conservatism, the latter by natural selection. But changes do creep in faster than the rate of genetic change, and cultures slowly evolve. Even that cultural dinosaur known as the Roman Catholic church—despite its claim to be the unchanging repository of truth and correct behavior—has changed greatly since its beginning.

Incidentally, it is at this hand ax stage of behavioral evolution at which most of the religions of today are still stuck. Our inflexible, absolutist moral codes also are fixated at this stage. The Ten Commandments are the moral counterpart of the "here's-how-you-rub-the-sticks-together" phase of technological evolution. If the only type of fire you want is one to heat your cave and cook your clams, the stick-rubbing method suffices. But if you want a fire to propel your jet airplane, some changes have to be made.

So, too, with the transmission of moral behavior. If we are to live lives which are as complex socially as jet airplanes are complex technologically, we need something more than the Ten Commandments. We cannot base our moral code upon arbitrary and capricious fiats reported to us by persons claiming to be privy to the intentions of the denizens of Sinai or Olympus. Our ethics can be based neither upon fictions concerning the nature of mankind nor upon fake reports concerning the desire of the deities. Our ethics must be firmly planted in the soil of scientific self-knowledge. They must be *improvable* and *adaptable*.

Where then, and with what, shall we begin?

The Principle of Enlightened Self-Interest

The principle of "enlightened self-interest" is an excellent first approximation to an ethical principle which is both consistent with what we know of human nature and is relevant to the problems of life in a complex society. Let us examine this principle.

Morality Is Rooted in Genetics

Can the cultural evolution of higher ethical values gain a direction and momentum of its own and completely replace genetic evolution? I think not. The genes hold culture on a leash. The leash is very long, but inevitably values will be constrained in accordance with their effects on the human gene pool. The brain is a product of evolution. Human behavior—like the deepest capacities for emotional response which drive and guide it—is the circuitous technique by which human genetic material has been and will be kept intact. Morality has no other demonstrable ultimate function.

Edward O. Wilson, *On Human Nature*, 1978.

First we must distinguish between "enlightened" and "unenlightened" self-interest. Let's take an extreme example for illustration. Suppose a person lived a totally selfish life of immediate gratification of every desire. Suppose that whenever someone else had something he wanted, he took it for himself.

It wouldn't be long at all before everyone would be up in arms against him, and he would have to spend all his waking hours fending off reprisals. Depending upon how outrageous his activity had been, he might very well lose his life in an orgy of neighborly revenge. The life of total but unenlightened self-interest might be exciting and pleasant as long as it lasts—but it is not likely to last long.

The person who practices "enlightened" self-interest, by contrast, is the person whose behavioral strategy simultaneously maximizes both the *intensity* and *duration* of personal gratification. An enlightened strategy will be one which, when practiced over a long span of time, will generate ever greater amounts and varieties of pleasures and satisfactions.

How is this to be done?

It is obvious that more is to be gained by cooperating with others than by acts of isolated egoism. One man with a rock cannot kill a buffalo for dinner. But a group of men or women, with a lot of rocks, can drive the beast off a cliff and—even after dividing the meat up among them—will still have more to eat than they would have had without cooperation.

Cooperation

But cooperation is a two-way street. If you cooperate with several others to kill buffalo, and each time they drive you away from the kill and eat it themselves, you will quickly take your services elsewhere, and you will leave the ingrates to stumble along without the Paleolithic equivalent of a fourth-for-bridge. Cooperation implies reciprocity.

Justice has its roots in the problem of determining fairness and reciprocity in cooperation. If I cooperate with you in tilling your field of corn, how much of the corn is due me at harvest time? When there is justice, cooperation operates at maximal efficiency, and the fruits of cooperation become ever more desirable. Thus, "enlightened self-interest" entails a desire for justice. With justice and with cooperation, we can have symphonies. Without it, we haven't even a song.

Because we have the nervous systems of social animals, we are generally happier in the company of our fellow creatures than alone. Because we are emotionally suggestible, as we practice enlightened self-interest, we usually will be wise to choose behaviors which will make others happy and willing to cooperate and accept us—for their happiness will reflect back upon us and intensify our own happiness. On the other hand, actions which harm others and make them unhappy—even if they do not trigger overt retaliation which decreases our happiness—will create an emotional milieu which, because of our suggestibility, will make us less happy.

Because our nervous systems are imprintable, we are able not only to fall in love at first sight, we are able to love objects and ideals as well as people. We are also able to love with variable intensities. Like the gosling attracted to the toy train, we are pulled forward by the desire for love. Unlike the gosling's "love," however, our love is to a considerable extent shapable by experience and is educable. A major aim of "enlightened self-interest," surely, is to give and receive love, both sexual and non-sexual. As a general—though not absolute—rule, we must choose those behaviors which will be likely to bring us love and acceptance, and we must eschew those behaviors which will not.

Another aim of enlightened self-interest is to seek beauty in all its forms, to preserve and prolong its resonance between the world outside and that within. Beauty and love are but different facets of the same jewel: Love is beautiful, and we love beauty.

The experience of love and beauty, however, is a *passive* function of the mind. How much greater is the joy which comes from creating beauty! How delicious it is to exercise *actively* our creative powers to engender that which can be loved! Paints and pianos are not necessarily prerequisites for the exercise of creativity: Whenever one transforms the raw materials of existence in such a way that he leaves them better than they were when he found them, he has been creative.

Conclusion

The task of moral education, then, is not to inculcate by rote great lists of do's and don'ts but rather to help people to predict the consequences of actions being considered. What are the long-term and immediate rewards and drawbacks of the acts? Will an act increase or decrease one's chances of experiencing the hedonic triad of love, beauty, and creativity?

Thus it happens, that when the Atheist approaches the problem of finding natural grounds for human morals and establishing a non-superstitious basis for behavior, it appears as though nature has already solved the problem to a great extent. Indeed, it appears as though the problem of establishing a natural, humanistic basis for ethical behavior is not much of a problem at all. It is in our natures to desire love, to seek beauty, and to thrill at the act of creation. The labyrinthine complexity we see when we examine traditional moral codes does not arise of necessity: It is largely the result of vain attempts to accommodate human needs and nature to the whimsical totems and taboos of the demons and deities who emerged with us from our cave dwellings at the end of the Paleolithic Era—and have haunted our houses ever since.

"In the twentieth century alone well over a hundred million persons have met a violent death at the hands of their fellow human beings."

The Holocaust Proves That Ordinary People Can Do Great Evil

Fred E. Katz

Fred. E. Katz grew up in Nazi Germany and lost many of his family members in the Holocaust. He has taught sociology in the United States and Israel. Katz is concerned that too often the great evils of the twentieth century (such as the Holocaust) are solely blamed on a few evil leaders (such as Hitler). Katz agrees that such leaders are responsible. However, Katz challenges his readers to consider how ordinary people, submitting to the expectations of their career paths, also contributed to the evils of the twentieth century. The remainder of Katz's book (not included in the viewpoint) supports this conclusion by quoting from journals of Nazi soldiers and officers who operated the death camps in World War II. The journals demonstrate that the need to survive, to be promoted, to do research, and to be successful drove the soldiers and officers to continue contributing to the evil.

As you read, consider the following questions:

1. Why does Katz want to take "evil" out of the context of the supernatural?
2. Why does Katz repeat the term "ordinary" so much in his writing?

Evil was not a topic we took seriously during my graduate-student days. Evil seemed to be of concern only to religious fundamentalists and professional philosophers, and not to those of us who were trying to understand people's social behavior scientifically. Hence one of history's major eruptions of evil, the Nazi Holocaust, was not included in our studies. I do not recall hearing the Holocaust mentioned in any of my classes. This pleased me. I did not want to hear about the Holocaust.

I am a Holocaust survivor. My parents and my brother did not survive. Yet from the time I discovered their fate, in 1946, I did no deliberate reading focused on the Holocaust for twenty-seven years. During this time I read none of that litany of Holocaust horrors which nowadays is all-too-familiar to most of us. To be sure I read daily newspapers and I heard newscasts on the radio. I was not out of touch with reality. And in a general sort of way I did know about the Holocaust, including information that came out at the war-crimes trials of some of the perpetrators. But I did not deliberately set out to investigate what had actually happened in the Holocaust.

More important, I made no effort to develop any kind of explanation beyond the then-existing conventional wisdom that here were horrors beyond the realm of understanding, that a singular group of monsters—led by Hitler—had been at work, and that a series of historical circumstances, including a great eruption of anti-Semitism, had culminated in an event that was as unfathomable as it was unique.

I did not consciously set out to remain ignorant about the Holocaust. My approach was largely subconscious. But my actions—of remaining so ignorant and so scientifically inactive—speak rather loudly. Here I was, a professional behavioral scientist who simply remained blind to the major horror of this century, a horror that had decimated my own family and forced me into a most turbulent and rudderless childhood and adolescence. . . .

Evil Defined

I define and use the word *evil* to mean behavior that deliberately deprives innocent people of their humanity, from small scale assaults on a person's dignity to outright murder. This is a *behavioral* definition of evil. It focuses on how people behave toward one another—where the behavior of one person, or an aggregate of persons, is destructive to others.

Evil is commonly seen in religious, moral and philosophical terms: as violating higher commandments, as breaking valued constraints that bind us to other persons, or as making us depart from a benign deity in favor of following a malignant deity, a satan. I do not deny that these are important, even profound ways of considering evil. I shall not delve into them because it would distract from what I want to accomplish here; namely showing that a behavioral view of evil helps us confront it. We thereby lift evil out of the realm of the supernatural and place it squarely in the realm of day-to-day living. . . .

Is Evil Real?

In the twentieth century alone well over a hundred million persons have met a violent death at the hands of their fellow human beings. This includes the military killings in the two World Wars, the deliberate annihilation of Jews by Nazis and Armenians by Turks, the bloodbaths during and after the Russian and Chinese Revolutions (the two revolutions are conservatively estimated to have produced 35 million deaths), and the killings in Cambodia and Biafra. It also includes deliberate mass starvation, most notably Stalin's program that starved to death some 14 million peasants in the early 1930s. This list is not complete, but it is surely long enough. Let us bear in mind that it does not include those who were maimed and continued their lives just short of death. Their number, too, runs into the millions.

If we accept my definition of evil, that it is behavior ranging from deliberate destruction of human dignity to deliberate destruction of human life, then evil is indeed real. And if extraordinary evil is defined as this kind of behavior on a huge scale, then this century has amassed a record of extraordinary evil.

There are two striking aspects to such evil. It is largely the handiwork of ordinary sorts of people; it is banal, as Hannah Arendt taught us. And, despite this, it is still very poorly understood. As a result we remain largely impotent in the face of extraordinary evil. Yet, I repeat, I believe we can reduce our impotence by improving our understanding of the processes that create evil.

Who Produces Extraordinary Evil?
Ordinary People, Like You and Me

Only a tiny proportion of this century's massive killings are attributable to the actions of those people we call criminals, or crazy people, or socially alienated people, or even, people we identify as evil people. The vast majority of killings were actually carried out by plain folk in the population—ordinary people, like you and me. Hence, in respect to mass killings, we must worry every bit as much about the actions of ordinary human beings as about the actions of crackpots and criminals.

What about the leaders? Does not the responsibility for evil rest with leaders who manipulate their people to do their bidding? Were not the Germans under the influence of Hitler? Were not the Soviets up to the early 1950s, under the influence of Stalin? Do not leaders cause their followers to do things that these followers do not really want to do?

Certainly the Hiders and Stalins of our world produced plans for evil that boggle the mind. But who transformed these plans into action? Ordinary people, like you and me. To begin with, who provides the fervor and zeal? Ordinary people, like you and me. Using Germany as an example, there people roared themselves hoarse and reached states of high ecstasy as they responded to Hitler's speeches. To Hitler and his cause they donated their energies, their skill, and their very lives, often doing so with joyful abandon. . . .

Who provides the quiet sustained effort, the plain hard work it takes to carry out huge programs of murderous action? Ordinary people, like you and me. The willing servants of Hitler, his foot soldiers, were ordinary Germans, not a specially selected cadre of fanatics.

How can one understand and, perhaps, forestall extraordinary evil? *By getting better understanding of how ordinary behavior can contribute to evil.*

To understand how extraordinary evil is planned, organized and carried out we need to look beyond the dreams and actions of human monsters, the Hitlers of the world. We need to look at *ordinary* behavior to understand *extraordinary* evil. The task is not easy. First we must overcome more of our traditional thinking about evil (in addition to the belief that only monsters produce evil, already mentioned). . . .

The Self Can Be a Prison

Where outward circumstances are not definitely unfortunate, a man should be able to achieve happiness, provided that his passions and interests are directed outward, not inward. It should be our endeavor, therefore, both in education and in attempts to adjust ourselves to the world, to aim at avoiding self-centered passions and at acquiring those affections and those interests which will prevent our thoughts from dwelling perpetually upon ourselves. It is not the nature of most men to be happy in a prison, and the passions which shut us up in ourselves constitute one of the worst kinds of prisons. Among such passions some of the commonest are fear, envy, the sense of sin, self-pity and self-admiration. In all these our desires are centered upon ourselves: there is no genuine interest in the outer world, but only a concern lest it should in some way injure us or fail to feed our ego.

Betrand Russell, *The Conquest of Happiness*, 1930.

Further on I shall illustrate a comparable personal career route—made up, also, of a sequence of seemingly small innocuous incremental steps—but leading to far cruder evil. I shall do so by examining in detail the history and career of Rudolf Hoess, the man in charge of the Auschwitz concentration camp.

The larger point is that such ordinary human behavior—as concentrating on one's career and adhering to the rules of a bureaucracy in which one works—can just as easily be used to participate in evil as in humane activities. But there are real gaps in our understanding of how this works. This book will try to fill some of these gaps. When we understand some ordinary behavior better we will be less surprised by evil, we will be less likely to be unwitting contributors to evil, we will be able to tell when we approach the threshold between good and evil, and we will be better equipped to forestall evil.

CHAPTER 5

What Should We Strive Toward?

Chapter Preface

Humans enjoy challenges. We may find ourselves attempting to run a faster mile, enrolling in a challenging college course, or building a taller skyscraper. Corresponding to our enjoyment of challenges is our dissatisfaction with our lives. Personal dissatisfaction is a common theme in all religions. It is also a theme running through psychotherapy, self-help books, diet programs, exercise programs, changing dress styles, and much of consumerism. In a similar way, when we look at our inner selves and at our beliefs, we often feel dissatisfied. We want to strive toward some higher standard of experience or knowledge. In this chapter, we will consider some of the ideals which writers have proposed for themselves and others.

A brief look at the life of Thomas Jefferson reveals how he strove to reach a number of higher goals. He was a leader in America's struggle for liberty. He was also active in science, agricultural research, and architecture. In the viewpoint by Jefferson, we find him writing a letter in which he challenges his nephew to reach for high goals. Jefferson believes that one should seek high moral standards, a well-rounded education, and a healthy body.

Ole Hallesby's viewpoint begins by explaining that humans have always been religious. Hallesby further points out that Jesus Christ was unique in the history of religious teachers. Hallesby writes that Jesus was the perfect example of divine love and wisdom. Thus, Jesus was the ultimate role-model for all humans. After examining the life of Jesus, Hallesby concludes that he and others should live as Jesus lived.

In contrast to the life of love which Jesus lived, Niccolo Machiavelli writes that we should rationally plot how we can be successful in the daily world of power, deceit, and political images. For Machiavelli, the goal of life should not be high moral standards. The goal of life is success in the social arena of power. With the acquisition and maintenance of power as our goal, we will rationally plan how to manipulate other people for our advantage.

The viewpoint by Benjamin Franklin contrasts sharply with Machiavelli's disregard for personal morals and introspection. Franklin is extremely focused on the morality of his personal thoughts and actions. In this viewpoint, Franklin shows no concern for social power. He is driven by a desire to reach perfection in his private life. He attempted, without success, to systematically develop a means to reach that goal. While admitting his failure, Franklin explains that the effort was worth it, because he did learn about his weaknesses.

Arnold Toynbee spent a lifetime studying history and world religions. He begins his viewpoint by observing that young people often ask what should guide their lives. Toynbee answers that we should live for love, creativity, and understanding. After explaining what he means by these terms, Toynbee concludes that if we seek these three qualities, our lives and the lives of those around us will be enriched.

> "*Give up money, give up fame, give up science, give [up] the earth itself and all it contains rather than do an immoral act.*"

Develop an Honest Heart

Thomas Jefferson

Thomas Jefferson was an architect, scientist, statesman, president, and author of the Declaration of Independence. His influence on the United States continues in many powerful ways today. One of the best ways to understand Jefferson is to study his many letters to friends and opponents. The following viewpoint is taken from a letter to Peter Carr, Jefferson's fifteen-year-old nephew and ward. In the letter, Jefferson urges Carr to grow intellectually, morally, and physically.

As you read, consider the following questions:
1. Jefferson lists many important things in life. What is first, second, and third on Jefferson's list? Why?
2. When a person is tempted to be dishonest or immoral, what does Jefferson suggest that the person do?
3. Jefferson compares physical exercise of a "limb" to moral exercise of one's character. Do you agree with this comparison? Why or why not?

From Thomas Jefferson's letter to his nephew and ward, Peter Carr, August 19, 1785.

Time now begins to be precious to you. Every day you lose, will retard a day your entrance on that public stage whereon you may begin to be useful to yourself. However the way to repair the loss is to improve the future time. I trust that with your dispositions even the acquisition of science is a pleasing employment. I can assure you that the possession of it is what (next to an honest heart) will above all things render you dear to your friends, and give you fame and promotion in your own country. When your mind shall be well improved with science, nothing will be necessary to place you in the highest points of view but to pursue the interests of your country, the interests of your friends, and your own interests also with the purest integrity, the most chaste honour. The defect of these virtues can never be made up by all the other acquirements of body and mind. Make these then your first object.

Develop an Honest Heart

Give up money, give up fame, give up science, give [up] the earth itself and all it contains rather than do an immoral act. And never suppose that in any possible situation or under any circumstances that it is best for you to do a dishonourable thing however slightly so it may appear to you. Whenever you are to do a thing tho' it can never be known but to yourself, ask yourself how you would act were all the world looking at you, and act accordingly. Encourage all your virtuous dispositions, and exercise them whenever an opportunity arises, being assured that they will gain strength by exercise as a limb of the body does, and that exercise will make them habitual. From the practice of the purest virtue you may be assured you will derive the most sublime comforts in every moment of life and in the moment of death. If ever you find yourself environed with difficulties and perplexing circumstances, out of which you are at a loss how to extricate yourself, do what is right, and be assured that that will extricate you the best out of the worst situations. Tho' you cannot see when you fetch one step, what will be the next, yet follow truth, justice, and plain-dealing, and never fear their leading you out of the labyrinth in the easiest manner possible. The knot which you thought a Gordian one will untie itself before you. Nothing is so mistaken as the supposition that a person is to extricate himself from a difficulty, by intrigue, by chicanery, by dissimulation, by trimming, by an untruth, by an injustice. This increases the difficulties tenfold, and those who pursue these methods, get themselves so involved at length that they can turn no way but their infamy becomes more exposed. It is of great importance to set a resolution, not to be shaken, never to tell an untruth. There is no vice so mean, so pitiful, so contemptible and he who permits himself to tell a lie once, finds it much easier to do it a second and third time, till at length it becomes habitual, he tells lies without attending to it, and truths without the world's believing him. This falsehood of the tongue leads to that of the heart, and in time depraves all its good dispositions.

Strengthen Your Moral Facilities

He who made us would have been a pitiful bungler if he had made the rules of our moral conduct a matter of science. For one man of science, there are thousands who are not. What would have become of them? Man was destined for society. His morality therefore was to be formed to this object. He was endowed with a sense of right and wrong merely relative to this. This sense is as much a part of his nature as the sense of hearing, seeing, feeling; it is the true foundation of morality. . . . The moral sense, or conscience, is as much a part of man as his leg or arm. It is given to all human beings in a stronger or weaker degree, as force of members is given them in a greater or less degree. It may be strengthened by exercise, as may any particular limb of the body . . . and/above all things lose no occasion of exercising your dispositions to be grateful, to be generous, to be charitable, to be humane, to be true, just, firm, orderly, couragious &c. Consider every act of this kind as an exercise which will strengthen your moral faculties, and increase your worth.

Thomas Jefferson in a letter to Peter Carr on August 10, 1787.

An honest heart being the first blessing, a knowing head is the second. It is time for you now to begin to be choice in your reading, to begin to pursue a regular course in it and not to suffer yourself to be turned to the right or left by reading anything out of that course. I have long ago digested a plan for you, suited to the circumstances in which you will be placed. This I will detail to you from time to time as you advance. For the present I advise you to begin a course of ancient history, reading every thing in the original and not in translations. First read Goldsmith's history of Greece. This will give you a digested view of that field. Then take up ancient history in the detail, reading the following books in the following order. Herodotus. Thucydides. Xenophontis Hellenica. Xenophontis Anabasis. Quintus Curtius. Justin. This shall form the first stage of your historical reading, and is all I need mention to you now. The next will be of Roman history. From that we will come down to Modern history. In Greek and Latin poetry, you have read or will read at school Virgil, Terence, Horace, Anacreon, Theocritus, Homer. Read also Milton's *Paradise Lost*, Ossian, Pope's works, Swift's works in order to form your style in your own language. In morality read Epictetus, Xenophontis' memorabilia, Plato's Socratic dialogues, Cicero's philosophies.

In order to assure a certain progress in this reading, consider what hours you have free from the school and the exercises of the school. Give about two of them every day to exercise; for health must not be sacrificed to learning. A strong body makes the mind strong. . . .

Never think of taking a book with you. The object of walking is to relax the mind. You should therefore not permit yourself even to think while you walk. But divert your attention by the objects surrounding you. Walking is the best possible exercise. Habituate yourself to walk very far. . . .

Our Moral Instinct

I sincerely, then, believe with you in the general existence of a moral instinct. I think it the brightest gem with which the human character is studded, and the want of it as more degrading than the most hideous of the bodily deformities.

Thomas Jefferson in a letter to Thomas Law on June 13, 1814.

There is no habit you will value so much as that of walking far without fatigue. I would advise you to take your exercise in the afternoon. Not because it is the best time for exercise for certainly it is not: but because it is the best time to spare from your studies; and habit will soon reconcile it to health, and render it nearly as useful as if you gave to that the more precious hours of the day. A little walk of half an hour in the morning when you first rise is advisable also. It shakes off sleep, and produces other good effects in the animal oeconomy. Rise at a fixed and an early hour, and go to bed at a fixed and early hour also. Sitting up late at night is injurious to the health, and not useful to the mind.

"He sought the welfare of others to such an extent that He was oblivious of Himself if only He might do some good to others."

Live for Others as Jesus Did

Ole Hallesby

Ole Hallesby was a leading Christian teacher and writer in Norway. In his book, *Why I Am a Christian*, Hallesby presents his reasons for choosing to follow Jesus. Hallesby explains that humans have continually sought to find the meaning of life in various religious systems. Yet, each system has been unsatisfactory in some way. Hallesby believes that Jesus is unique in the history of religion because Jesus' life was the expression of how humans were meant to live. Hallesby believes that Jesus' legacy of service to others is the most satisfying model for humans.

As you read, consider the following questions:

1. According to Hallesby, how was Jesus different from other religious leaders in history?
2. What is the relationship between Hallesby's conscience and the life style of Jesus?
3. Why does Hallesby say that he would be untrue to himself if he rejected Jesus?

Excerpted from *Why I Am a Christian*, by Ole Hallesby (Minneapolis: Augsburg Publishing House, 1930). Reprinted with permission.

Human life has its own peculiar characteristics, which make it human. And this life develops only under certain conditions and in certain environments.

One of the characteristics of human life, among others, is that it must discover its own peculiarity, that is, discover the meaning of life. In all other living beings the innate life unfolds itself automatically, by means of the instincts. In man, however, the unfolding of life takes place consciously and deliberately.

Man himself must know what it means to be a man, and will to be it. He himself must select the environment in which his own peculiar life can unfold itself. And this is what men have been working at down through the ages as far back as we have any historical records of human life. The best men and women of each generation have been the ones who have sacrificed the most time and energy to ascertain the meaning of life.

The Founding of Religions

One day a quiet, good man came forth and said: "I have found it."

Men crowded around him and listened. After they had heard him to the end, they said: "Verily, we have found it!"

And a religion had been founded upon earth.

Now, all life is supplied with a peculiar apparatus which we call sensitiveness or feeling. It constitutes a very important factor in life. It serves life both positively and negatively. It serves positively by making the living organism aware of those things or conditions which will promote its existence. Even in plants we can clearly discern a "sensitiveness" of this kind. If a tree, for instance, is growing in lean earth and there is better earth a short distance away, we notice that the tree practically moves away from the lean earth by sending its roots over into the good earth.

The feelings serve the living organism negatively by making it aware of everything in its surroundings which is detrimental to its existence. Thus, for instance, the sensitiveness of our skin. It helps us to protect our bodies against dangerous cold or heat. If we touch a hot iron, our feelings give instant warning and we withdraw our hand, thereby escaping greater injury. . . .

Our soul-life, too, has its apparatus for feeling, the function of which is to serve this life by pointing out those things in our environment which are conducive to the well being of the soul and by warning against those things which are detrimental to it. This apparatus of the soul we usually call the conscience. It is a part of that life which is peculiar to man, and a very important part, because it is the life-preserving and life-protecting function of the soul.

The Loss of Self

The cult of "I," has taken hold with the strength and impetus of a new religion. But the joker in the pack is that it is all based on a false idea. . . .

A long time ago, in a book called *Civilization and Its Discontents* Freud pointed out that there is an unresolvable conflict between the human being's selfish, primitive, infantile impulses and the restraint he or she must impose on those impulses if a stable society is to be maintained. The "self" is not a handsome god or goddess waiting coyly to be revealed. On the contrary, its complexity, confusion and mystery have proved so difficult that throughout the ages men and women have talked gratefully about losing themselves. They lose the self in contemplating a great work of art, or in nature, or in scientific research, or in writing poetry, or in fashioning things with their hands or in projects that will benefit others rather than themselves.

The current glorification of self-love will turn out in the end to be a no-win proposition, because in questions of personality or "identity," what counts is not who you are, but what you do. "By their fruits, ye shall know them." And by their fruits, they shall know themselves.

Margaret Halsey, "What's Wrong with 'Me, Me, Me,'" *Newsweek*, April 17, 1978.

Its task is to prove all things both from without and within which affect our spiritual life and to determine whether they are beneficial or detrimental to the soul. If the conscience is permitted to function normally, nothing reaches the soul before the conscience has expressed its opinion concerning it.

When the quiet, good man had spoken, and men had heard from him what the meaning of life was, conscience immediately began its work. It proved all things. But gradually the number of those grew greater and greater who said to themselves and later to others: this is not the meaning of life.

And they began anew to try to find the answer to the old problem.

One day another man came forth. He, too, was a quiet and a good man. He, too, said: "I have found it."

And people listened and said: "In truth, now we have found it."

And another new religion had been founded on earth.

Thus it continued through hundreds and thousands of years. But the conscience of man was not satisfied with any of the solutions.

Then Came Jesus

Then came Jesus.

He showed us what the meaning of life is. When Jesus came, we saw for the first time on earth what a real man is. He called himself the *"Son of Man."*

The others, who had preceded Jesus, could only tell us how a man should be. Jesus, however, exemplified it in His own life. He did not only point out the ideal, as others had done; He Himself was the ideal, and He actually lived it out before our very eyes.

Permit me to mention two things in connection with this ideal. In the first place, Jesus, too, directs His appeal to our consciences. Furthermore, He seeks no other following but that which the consciences of men will grant Him.

Many think that Jesus forces men to follow Him. In so doing they reveal how little they know about Him.

Let me call your attention to one incident in the life of Jesus. It was during the great awakening in Galilee. The people were streaming together and almost trampling one another down. One day Jesus stopped and looked at all these people. And He seemed to ask Himself this question: I wonder if they have understood me? Then He turned and cried out once again to the multitudes: "No man can be my disciple without renouncing all that he hath, yea, even his own life" (Luke 14:25–33).

A man who speaks to the people in that way does not expect to gain any other adherents but such as are convinced in their hearts that both the man and his message are trustworthy and that they, therefore, are inwardly bound to follow him, regardless of what it may cost them.

This is the remarkable thing that happens. When our consciences are confronted by Jesus, we are compelled to ac-

What Did Jesus Say About Himself?

Among the religious leaders who have attained a large following throughout history, Jesus Christ is unique in the fact that He alone claimed to be God in human flesh. A common misconception is that some or many of the leaders of the world's religions made similar claims, but this is simply not the case.

Buddha did not claim to be God; Moses never said that he was Yahweh; Mohammed did not identify himself as Allah; and nowhere will you find Zoroaster claiming to be Ahura Mazda. Yet Jesus, the carpenter from Nazareth, said that he who has seen Him (Jesus) has seen the Father (John 14:9).

The claims of Christ are many and varied. He said that He existed before Abraham (John 8:58), and that He was equal with the Father (John 5:17, 18). Jesus claimed the ability to forgive sins (Mark 2:5–7), which the Bible teaches was something that God alone could do (Isaiah 43:25).

The New Testament equated Jesus as the creator of the universe (John 1:3), and that He is the one who holds everything together (Colossians 1:17). The apostle Paul says that God was manifest in the flesh (I Timothy 3:16, KJV), and John the evangelist says that "the Word was God" (John 1:1). The united testimony of Jesus and the writers of the New Testament is that He was more than mere man; He *was* God.

Not only did His friends notice that He claimed to be God, but so did His enemies as well. There may be some doubt today among the skeptics who refuse to examine the evidence, but there was no doubt on the part of the Jewish authorities.

When Jesus asked them why they wanted to stone Him, they replied, "For a good work we do not stone You, but for blasphemy; and because You, being a man, make Yourself out to be God" (John 10:33, NASB).

This fact separates Jesus from the other religious figures. In the major religions of the world, the teachings—not the teacher—are all-important.

Josh McDowall and Don Stewart, *Answers to Tough Questions*, 1980.

cord Him our full and unqualified approval. At least, He received the approval of my conscience. No matter in what situation I see Jesus, my conscience says: Verily, that is the way a man should be. . . .

Jesus Lived for Others

What, then, was the life of Jesus like?

Large volumes, both scientific and devotional, have, of course, been written about this. I must be brief and shall, therefore, mention only a couple of the fundamental traits, the two which, to my mind, most clearly distinguish the life of Jesus from that of all other people.

In the first place, Jesus never had to grope His way to find the meaning of life, as everybody else has had to do, both before and after His time. Unerringly He discerned it and lived in harmony with it, to Him a perfectly natural way of living. We can not discover that He was ever in doubt, not even during His temptation or His passion.

The unique thing about Jesus, however, that which impresses us most, was, without comparison, His intimate and unbroken fellowship with the Father. He Himself knew that this was the secret of his life. . . .

In the second place, I would mention the life Jesus lived among men.

The unique thing about this aspect of His life, as contrasted with our lives, was that He sought the welfare of others to such an extent that He was oblivious of Himself if only He might do some good to others.

Jesus has had many enemies, both among His contemporaries and since, and they have scrutinized His life very closely. None of them, however, has been able to point to a single instance in which Jesus acted from selfish motives.

Jesus has given expression to this normal human life by saying: "Thou shalt love the Lord thy God above all else, and thy neighbor as thyself.". . .

I Had to Choose

Permit me at this point to mention the two things which came to mean most to me.

In the first place, concerning the life of Jesus with which I had now come in contact, my conscience compelled me to say: Verily, that is the way a man should be. I began to feel also that the life of Jesus was a condemnation of my own life. . . .

I now saw how inhuman the life was which I had been living. Jesus lived His life for others. I had lived my whole life for myself, in petty selfishness, pride, and pleasure. . . .

In the second place, the life of Jesus attracted me with a power which I had never before felt in all my life.

I saw before my eyes that pure, good, beautiful, and strong life which God had intended that I should live. It attracted me with a wonderful power.

I could understand now why so many young men were drawn to Jesus. All He had to say to them was: "Follow me," and they left all and followed Him. . . .

Jesus once said: "Everyone that is of the truth heareth my voice." Now I knew that Jesus was right. Every one who is confronted by Jesus and refuses to accept Him is untrue to himself.

I had formerly believed that people who became Christians had to deny their own convictions, if they were people who did their own thinking, but now I saw that I had to become a Christian if I was not to be untrue to myself and my most sacred convictions.

Then came the choice.

I had to choose. . . .

I could not endure being untrue to myself, both for time and for eternity. I could not enter upon a life of unequivocal falsehood, such as would have been the case if, after having been confronted with Jesus, I had continued to live as before.

So I chose to follow Jesus.

> *"If men were all good, this precept would not be a good one; but as they are bad, and would not observe their faith with you, so you are not bound to keep faith with them."*

Be Powerful

Niccolo Machiavelli

Niccolo Machiavelli (1469–1527) held various government positions in Florence, Italy, when the Medici family was in power. *The Prince*, from which this viewpoint is taken, is his most famous book. Machiavelli writes to give advice to a prince (or any ruler) about the realities of politics. Beginning with the assumption that the only goal of a prince is to gain and maintain power, Machiavelli suggests using honesty, deceit, love, cruelty, religious values, and hypocrisy to reach the goal of power. In other words, the acquisition and maintenance of power should not be based upon moral principles, but upon expedience.

As you read, consider the following questions:

1. Machiavelli writes that many imaginary kingdoms and imaginary rules of politics can be found in books, but he is going to discuss the truth of the matter. What is the relationship between idealism and realism in values, personal goals, and politics?
2. In the passage, the author creates a contrast between fear and love. Is it true that a ruler can maintain control over people through fear, but not through appealing to love and voluntary commitment?
3. Machiavelli assumes that all people are selfish and evil. He concludes that it would be self-destructive to be good and kind in the real world. Do you agree or disagree? Why?

Reprinted from *The Prince*, by Niccolo Machiavelli, translated by Luigi Ricci (New York: Random House, 1950).

It now remains to be seen what are the methods and rules for a prince as regards his subjects and friends. And as I know that many have written of this, I fear that my writing about it may be deemed presumptuous, differing as I do, especially in this matter, from the opinions of others. But my intention being to write something of use to those who understand, it appears to me more proper to go to the real truth of the matter than to its imagination; and many have imagined republics and principalities which have never been seen or known to exist in reality; for how we live is so far removed from how we ought to live, that he who abandons what is done for what ought to be done, will rather learn to bring about his own ruin than his preservation. A man who wishes to make a profession of goodness in everything must necessarily come to grief among so many who are not good. Therefore it is necessary for a prince, who wishes to maintain himself, to learn how not to be good, and to use this knowledge and not use it, according to the necessity of the case.

Facing Reality

Leaving on one side, then, those things which concern only an imaginary prince, and speaking of those that are real, I state that all men, and especially princes, who are placed at a greater height, are reputed for certain qualities which bring them either praise or blame. Thus one is considered liberal, another *misero* or miserly; . . . one cruel, another merciful; one a breaker of his word, another trustworthy; one effeminate and pusillanimous, another fierce and high-spirited; one humane, another haughty; one lascivious, another chaste; one frank, another astute; one hard, another easy; one serious, another frivolous; one religious, another an unbeliever, and so on. I know that every one will admit that it would be highly praiseworthy in a prince to possess all the above-named qualities that are reputed good, but as they cannot all be possessed or observed, human conditions not permitting of it, it is necessary that he should be prudent enough to avoid the scandal of those vices which would lose him the state, and guard himself if possible against those which will not lose it him, but if not able to, he can indulge them with less scruple. And yet he must not mind incurring the scandal of those vices, without which it would be difficult to save the state, for if one considers well, it will be found that some things which seem virtues would, if followed, lead to one's ruin, and some others which appear vices result in one's greater security and wellbeing. . . .

Love or Fear as Motives

From this arises the question whether it is better to be loved more than feared, or feared more than loved. The reply is, that one ought to be both feared and loved, but as it is difficult for the two to go together, it is much safer to be feared than loved, if one of the two has to be wanting. For it may be said of men in general that they are ungrateful, voluble, dissemblers, anxious to avoid danger, and covetous of gain; as long as you benefit them, they are entirely yours; they offer you their blood, their goods, their life, and their children, as I have before said, when the necessity is remote; but when it approaches, they revolt. And the prince who has relied solely on their words, without making other preparations, is ruined; for the friendship which is gained by purchase and not through grandeur and nobility of spirit is bought but not secured, and at a pinch is not to be expended in your service. And men have less scruple in offending one who makes himself loved than one who makes himself feared; for love is held by a chain of obligation which, men being selfish, is broken whenever it serves their purpose; but fear is maintained by a dread of punishment which never fails.

Still, a prince should make himself feared in such a way that if he does not gain love, he at any rate avoids hatred; for fear and the absence of hatred may well go together, and will be always attained by one who abstains from interfering with the property of his citizens and subjects or with their women. And when he is obliged to take the life of any one, let him do so when there is a proper justification and manifest reason for it; but above all he must abstain from taking the property of others, for men forget more easily the death of their father than the loss of their patrimony [inheritance]. . . .

But when the prince is with his army and has a large number of soldiers under his control, then it is extremely necessary that he should not mind being thought cruel; for without this reputation he could not keep an army united or disposed to any duty. Among the noteworthy actions of Hannibal is numbered this, that although he had an enormous army, composed of men of all nations and fighting in foreign countries, there never arose any dissension either among them or against the prince, either in good fortune or in bad. This could not be due to anything but his inhuman cruelty, which together with his infinite other virtues, made him always venerated and terrible in the sight of his soldiers, and without it his other virtues would not have sufficed to produce that effect. Thoughtless writers admire on the one hand his actions, and on the other blame the principal cause of them. . . .

I conclude, therefore, with regard to being feared and loved, that men love at their own free will, but fear at the will of the prince, and that a wise prince must rely on what is in his power and not on what is in the power of others, and he must only contrive to avoid incurring hatred, as has been explained.

Honesty and Trickery

How laudable it is for a prince to keep good faith and live with integrity, and not with astuteness, every one knows. Still, the experience of our times shows those princes to have done great things who have had little regard for good faith, and have been able by astuteness to confuse men's brains, and who have ultimately overcome those who have made loyalty their foundation. . . .

A prince being thus obliged to know well how to act as a beast must imitate the fox and the lion, for the lion cannot protect himself from traps, and the fox cannot defend himself from wolves. One must therefore be a fox to recognise traps, and a lion to frighten wolves. Those that wish to be only lions do not understand this. Therefore, a prudent ruler ought not to keep faith when by so doing it would be against his interest, and when the reasons which made him bind himself no longer exist. If men were all good, this precept would not be a good one; but as they are bad, and would not observe their faith with you, so you are not bound to keep faith with them. Nor have legitimate grounds ever failed a prince who wished to show colourable excuse for the non-fulfilment of his promise. Of this one could furnish an infinite number of modern examples, and show how many times peace has been broken, and how many promises rendered worthless, by the faithlessness of princes, and those that have been best able to imitate the fox have succeeded best. But it is necessary to be able to disguise this character well, and to be a great feigner and dissembler; and men are so simple and so ready to obey present necessities, that one who deceives will always find those who allow themselves to be deceived.

Hagar the Horrible; reprinted by permission of King Features Syndicate, Inc.

I will only mention one modern instance. Alexander VI did nothing else but deceive men, he thought of nothing else, and found the occasion for it; no man was ever more able to give assurances, or affirmed things with stronger oaths, and no man observed them less; however, he always succeeded in his deceptions, as he well knew this aspect of things.

Tools of Success

It is not, therefore, necessary for a prince to have all the above-named qualities, but it is very necessary to seem to have them. I would even be bold to say that to possess them and always to observe them is dangerous, but to appear to possess them is useful. Thus it is well to seem merciful, faithful, humane, sincere, religious, and also to be so; but you must have the mind so disposed that when it is needful to be otherwise you may be able to change to the opposite qualities. And it must be understood that a prince, and especially a new prince, cannot observe all those things which are considered good in men, being often obliged, in order to maintain the state, to act against faith, against charity, against humanity, and against religion. And, therefore, he must have a mind disposed to adapt itself according to the wind, and as the variations of fortune dictate, and, as I said before, not deviate from what is good, if possible, but be able to do evil if constrained.

A prince must take great care that nothing goes out of his mouth which is not full of the above-named five qualities, and, to see and hear him, he should seem to be all mercy, faith, integrity, humanity, and religion. And nothing is more necessary than to seem to have this last quality, for men in general judge more by the eyes than by the hands, for every one can see, but very few have to feel. Everybody sees what you appear to be, few feel what you are, and those few will not dare to oppose themselves to the many, who have the majesty of the state to defend them; and in the actions of men, and especially of princes, from which there is no appeal, the end justifies the means. Let a prince therefore aim at conquering and maintaining the state, and the means will always be judged honourable and praised by every one, for the vulgar is always taken by appearances and the issue of the event; and the world consists only of the vulgar, and the few who are not vulgar are isolated when the many have a rallying point in the prince. A certain prince of the present time, whom it is well not to name, never does anything but preach peace and good faith, but he is really a great enemy to both, and either of them, had he observed them, would have lost him state or reputation on many occasions.

> "*It was about this time I conceived the bold and arduous project of arriving at moral perfection. I wished to live without committing any fault at any time.*"

Aim for Personal Perfection

Benjamin Franklin

Benjamin Franklin (1706–1790) was a journalist, business-man, scientist, statesman, educator, and leader in the establishment of the United States. He grew up in a religious home, but was not a religious person himself. This viewpoint is taken from his autobiography. In it, Franklin tells how he decided to develop and follow a program to reach moral perfection. His goal is complete self-control.

As you read, consider the following questions:

1. What is Franklin's point in telling the story of the "speckled axe"?
2. A friendly Quaker suggested that Franklin add humility to the list of virtues. Do you believe that Franklin reached the goal of humility?
3. What does Franklin mean when he writes, "I cannot boast of much success in acquiring the *reality* of this virtue [humility], but I had a good deal with regard to the *appearance* of it."

From *The Autobiography of Benjamin Franklin* (Boston: Houghton Mifflin, 1903).

It was about this time I conceived the bold and arduous project of arriving at moral perfection. I wished to live without committing any fault at any time; I would conquer all that either natural inclination, custom, or company might lead me into. As I knew, or thought I knew, what was right and wrong, I did not see why I might not always do the one and avoid the other. But I soon found I had undertaken a task of more difficulty than I had imagined. While my care was employed in guarding against one fault, I was often surprised by another; habit took the advantage of inattention; inclination was sometimes too strong for reason. I concluded, at length, that the mere speculative conviction that it was our interest to be completely virtuous was not sufficient to prevent our slipping; and that the contrary habits must be broken and good ones acquired and established before we can have any dependence on a steady, uniform rectitude of conduct. For this purpose I therefore contrived the following method. . . .

Virtues to Acquire

I concluded under thirteen names of virtues all that at that time occurred to me as necessary or desirable and annexed to each a short precept which fully expressed the extent I gave to its meaning.

These names of virtues with their precepts were:

1. TEMPERANCE
Eat not to dullness; drink not to elevation.

2. SILENCE
Speak not but what may benefit others or yourself; avoid trifling conversation.

3. ORDER
Let all your things have their places; let each part of your business have its time.

4. RESOLUTION
Resolve to perform what you ought; perform without fail what you resolve.

5. FRUGALITY
Make no expense but to do good to others or yourself; i.e., waste nothing.

6. INDUSTRY

Lose no time; be always employed in something useful; cut off all unnecessary actions.

7. SINCERITY

Use no harmful deceit; think innocently and justly, and, if you speak, speak accordingly.

8. JUSTICE

Wrong none by doing injuries or omitting the benefits that are your duty.

9. MODERATION

Avoid extremes; forbear resenting injuries so much as you think they deserve.

10. CLEANLINESS

Tolerate no uncleanliness in body, clothes or habitation.

11. TRANQUILLITY

Be not disturbed at trifles, or at accidents common or unavoidable.

12. CHASTITY

Rarely use venery but for health or offspring, never to dullness, weakness, or the injury of your own or another's peace or reputation.

13. HUMILITY

Imitate Jesus and Socrates.

My intention being to acquire the *habitude* of all these virtues, I judged it would be well not to distract my attention by attempting the whole at once, but to fix it on one of them at a time; and, when I should be master of that, then to proceed to another, and so on, till I should have gone through the thirteen; and, as the previous acquisition of some might facilitate the acquisition of certain others, I arranged them with that view as they stand above. Temperance first, as it tends to procure that coolness and clearness of head which is so necessary where constant vigilance was to be kept up and guard maintained against the unremitting attraction of ancient habits and the force of perpetual temptations. This being acquired and established, Silence would be more easy; and my desire being to gain knowledge at the same time that I improved in virtue, and considering that in conversation it was obtained rather by the use of the ears than of the tongue, and therefore wishing to break a habit I was getting into of prattling, punning, and joking which only made me acceptable to trifling company, I gave Silence the second place. This and the next, Order, I expected would allow me more time for attending to my project and my studies. Resolution, once become habitual, would keep me firm in my endeavors to obtain all the subsequent virtues; Frugality and Industry freeing me from my remaining debt, and producing affluence and independence, would make more easy the practice of Sincerity and Justice, etc., etc. Conceiving then that agreeably to the advice of Pythagoras in his Golden Verses daily examination would be necessary, I contrived the following method for conducting that examination.

I made a little book in which I allotted a page for each of the virtues. I ruled each page with red ink so as to have seven columns, one for each day of the week, marking each column with a letter for the day. I crossed these columns with thirteen red lines, marking the beginning of each line with the first letter of one of the virtues, on which line and in its proper column I might mark by a little black spot, every fault I found upon examination to have been committed respecting that virtue upon that day.

I determined to give a week's strict attention to each of the virtues successively. Thus in the first week my great guard was to avoid even the least offense against Temperance, leaving the other virtues to their ordinary chance, only marking every evening the faults of the day. Thus, if in the first week I could keep my first line, marked T, clear of spots, I supposed the habit of that virtue so much strengthened and its opposite weakened that I might venture extending my attention to include the next, and for the following week keep both lines clear of spots. Proceeding thus to the last, I could go through a course complete in thirteen weeks and four courses in a year. . . .

Ordering My Day

The precept of Order requiring that *every part of my business should have its allotted time*, one page in my little book contained the following scheme of employment for the twenty-four hours of a natural day.

The Morning.	5	Rise, wash, and address *Powerful Goodness!* Contrive day's business and take the resolution of the day; prosecute the present study, and breakfast.
Question. What good shall I do this day?	6	
	7	
	8	
	9	Work.
	10	
	11	
Noon.	12	Read, or overlook my accounts, and dine.
	1	
	2	
	3	
	4	Work.
	5	
Evening.	6	Put things in their places. Supper. Music or diversion, or conversation. Examination of the day.
Question. What good have I done to-day?	7	
	8	
	9	
	10	
	11	
	12	
Night.	1	Sleep
	2	
	3	
	4	

I entered upon the execution of this plan for self-examination and continued it with occasional intermissions for some time. I was surprised to find myself so much fuller of faults than I had imagined; but I had the satisfaction of seeing them diminish. To avoid the trouble of renewing now and then my little book, which, by scraping out the marks on the paper of old faults to make room for new ones in a new course, became full of holes, I transferred my tables and precepts to the ivory leaves of a memorandum book on which the lines were drawn with red ink that made a durable stain, and on those lines I marked my faults with a black-lead pencil, which marks I could easily wipe out with a wet sponge. After a while I went through one course only in a year, and afterward only one in several years, till at length I omitted them entirely, being employed in voyages and business abroad with a multiplicity of affairs that interfered; but I always carried my little book with me.

A Speckled Axe Was Best

My scheme of Order gave me the most trouble. . . . I was almost ready to give up the attempt and content myself with a faulty character in that respect, like the man who, in buying an axe of a smith, my neighbor, desired to have the whole of its surface as bright as the edge. The smith consented to grind it bright for him if he would turn the wheel; he turned while the smith pressed the broad face of the axe hard and heavily on the stone, which made the turning of it very fatiguing. The man came every now and then from the wheel to see how the work went on, and at length would take his axe as it was, without farther grinding. "No," said the smith, "turn on, turn on: we shall have it bright by-and-by; as yet, it is only speckled." "Yes, " says the man, *but I think I like a speckled axe best.*". . .

In truth, I found myself incorrigible with respect to Order; and now I am grown old and my memory bad, I feel very sensibly the want of it. But on the whole, though I never arrived at the perfection I had been so ambitious of obtaining, but fell far short of it, yet I was by the endeavor a better and a happier man than I otherwise should have been if I had not attempted it.

I Added Humility to My List

My list of virtues contained at first but twelve; but a Quaker friend having kindly informed me that I was generally thought proud; that my pride showed itself frequently in conversation; that I was not content with being in the right when discussing any point, but was overbearing, and rather insolent, of which he convinced me by mentioning several instances; I determined endeavoring to cure myself, if I could, of this vice or folly among the rest, and I added Humility to my list, giving an extensive meaning to the word.

Franklin's Log and Virtues

	S.	M.	T.	W.	T.	F.	S.
TEMPERANCE. EAT NOT TO DULLNESS; DRINK NOT TO ELEVATION.							
T.							
S.	*	*		*		*	
O.	**	*	*		*	*	*
R.			*			*	
F.		*			*		
I.			*				
S.							
J.							
M.							
C.							
T.							
C.							
H.							

These names of virtues with their precepts were:

TEMPERANCE
Eat not to dullness. Drink not to elevation.

SILENCE
Speak not but what may benefit others or yourself. Avoid trifling conversation.

ORDER
Let all your things have their places. Let each part of your business have its time.

RESOLUTION
Resolve to perform what you ought. Perform without fail what you resolve.

FRUGALITY
Make no expense but to do good to others or yourself; i.e., waste nothing.

INDUSTRY
Lose no time. Be always employed in something useful. Cut off all unnecessary actions.

SINCERITY
Use no hurtful deceit Think innocently and justly; and, if you speak, speak accordingly.

JUSTICE
Wrong none by doing injuries or omitting the benefits that are your duty.

MODERATION
Avoid extremes. Forbear resenting injuries so much as you think they deserve.

CLEANLINESS
Tolerate no uncleanliness in body, clothes or habitation.

TRANQUILLITY
Be not disturbed at trifles or at accidents common or unavoidable.

CHASTITY
Rarely use venery but for health or offspring—never to dullness, weakness, or the injury of your own or another's peace or reputation.

HUMILITY
Imitate Jesus and Socrates.

I cannot boast of much success in acquiring the *reality* of this virtue, but I had a good deal with regard to the *appearance* of it. I made it a rule to forbear all direct contradiction to the sentiments of others and all positive assertion of my own. I even forbade myself, agreeably to the old laws of our Junto, the use of every word or expression in the language that imported a fixed opinion, such as "certainly," "undoubtedly," etc., and I adopted, instead of them, "I conceive," "I apprehend," or "I imagine" a thing to be so or so; or it "so appears to me at present." When another asserted something that I thought an error, I denied myself the pleasure of contradicting him abruptly and of showing immediately some absurdity in his proposition; and in answering I began by observing that in certain cases or circumstances his opinion would be right, but in the present case there *appeared* or *seemed* to me some difference, etc. I soon found the advantage of this change in my manner; the conversations I engaged in went on more pleasantly. The modest way in which I proposed my opinions procured them a readier reception and less contradiction; I had less mortification when I was found to be in the wrong, and I more easily prevailed with others to give up their mistakes and join with me when I happened to be in the right. . . .

In reality there is, perhaps, no one of our natural passions so hard to subdue as Pride. Disguise it, struggle with it, beat it down, stifle it, mortify it as much as one pleases, it is still alive, and will every now and then peep out and show itself; you will see it, perhaps, often in this history; for even if I could conceive that I had completely overcome it, I should probably be proud of my humility.

| "*Man should live for loving, for understanding, and for creating.*"

Seek Love, Creation, and Understanding

Arnold Toynbee

Arnold Toynbee (1889–1975) was director of studies in the Royal Institute of International Affairs and professor of history at London University. He became internationally famous for his multi-volume work, *A Study of History*, that traced the rise and fall of civilizations throughout history. His main interest in the latter part of his life was religion as a means to world unity. In this viewpoint, Toynbee discusses why humans should make understanding, love, and creativity the ultimate goals in life. Toynbee also values self-sacrifice and rationality.

As you read, consider the following questions:
1. Why does Toynbee assume that self-sacrifice is a normal part of commitment?
2. When Toynbee uses the term "love," what does he mean?
3. What does Toynbee mean when he writes, "the whole of human life is a struggle to keep the reason uppermost"?

The confusion, strain, pressures, complications, and rapid changes in contemporary life are having their effect all over the world, and they are particularly disturbing for the young. The young want to find their way, to understand the meaning of life, to cope with the circumstances with which they are confronted. What should man live for? This question is particularly acute for the young, but it haunts everyone at every stage of life.

I would say that man should live for loving, for understanding, and for creating. I think man should spend all his ability and all his strength on pursuing all these three aims, and he should sacrifice himself, if necessary, for the sake of achieving them. Anything worthwhile may demand self-sacrifice, and, if you think it worthwhile, you will be prepared to make the sacrifice.

Live for Love

I myself believe that love does have an absolute value, that it is what gives value to human life, and also to the life of some other species of mammals and birds. I can think of some birds and mammals, besides ourselves, that live for love. I also believe (I know that this cannot be demonstrated) that love, as we know it by direct experience in living creatures on this planet, is also present as a spiritual presence behind the universe. Love can and does sometimes bring out responsive love, as we know in our own human experience, and, when that happens, love spreads and expands itself. But love may also meet with hostility, and then it will call for self-sacrifice, which may seem sometimes to be in vain. All the same, love, if it is strong enough, will move us to sacrifice ourselves, even if we see no prospect that this self-sacrifice will win a victory by transforming hostility into love. The only way in which love can conquer is by changing the state of feeling, the state of mind, of some other person from hostility to an answering love. I believe, though it is hard of course for any of us to live up to this belief, that the lead given by love ought to be followed at all costs, whatever the consequences. I think that love is the only spiritual power that can overcome the self-centeredness that is inherent in being alive. Love is the only thing that makes life possible, or, indeed, tolerable.

I had better say, before I go on, a few words about what I mean by love. This is so important, as I see it, that I want to make the meaning of the word love, as I use the word, clear, because, at any rate in English, this word 'love' is ambiguous. I can say 'I love whisky', or 'I love sexual relations', or 'I love chocolate'; that is not the kind of love that I mean. Or I can say 'I love my wife', or 'I love my children', or 'I love my fellow human beings', or 'I love God'. . . .

True love is an emotion which discharges itself in an activity that overcomes self-centeredness by expending the self on people and on purposes beyond the self. It is an outward-going spiritual movement from the self toward the universe and toward the ultimate spiritual reality behind the universe.

Love Is the Key

Love is the key to a fulfilling life: love yourselves; love others; love truth, goodness, and beauty; love nature—the trees, the flowers, the sky, the stars. If you feel love, then you will be able to be compassionate with yourselves and with others. Being compassionate, you will be tolerant and respectful. Being tolerant and respectful, you will be nonviolent. This attitude will elicit love, compassion, tolerance, and respect from others. Then you will feel a special happiness, together with a sense of peace and well-being.

Al-Abdin in *Letters to Young People*, 1989.

There is a paradox here. This love that is a form of self-denial is the only true self-fulfillment, as has been pointed out by the founders of all the great historic religions. It is self-fulfillment because this outward-going love reintegrates the self into the ultimate spiritual reality of which the self is a kind of splinter that has been temporarily separated and alienated. The self seeks to fulfill itself, and it seeks blindly to fulfill itself by exploiting the universe. But the only way in which it can fulfill itself truly is to unite itself with the spiritual reality behind the universe, so this outgoing love, which is a form of reunion, a union with other people and with ultimate spiritual reality, is the true form of fulfillment. . . .

Man is a social being, and therefore, among all the objects for his love that there are in the universe and beyond it, he ought, I suppose, to love his fellow human beings first and foremost. But he should also love all non-human living creatures, animals, and plants, as well, because they are akin to man; they too are branches of the great tree of life. This tree has a common root; we do not know where the root comes from, but we do know that we all spring from it. Man should also love inanimate nature, because this, too, is part of the universe which is mankind's habitat.

I think people in India and Eastern Asia have a greater wish, and a greater sense of the need, to love non-human living creatures, and also inanimate nature, than people in the Western world have. This wish to expand the field of human love is not so strong in the Western tradition. By Western I do not mean just Christian: I mean Christian and Jewish and Muslim, because Christianity and Islam are derivatives, offshoots, of Judaism. However, in the Western tradition, too, there are traces of this feeling for nature. For instance, Saint Francis of Assisi, one of the greatest religious figures in Western history so far, has written, in the earliest surviving piece of Italian poetry, a hymn in which he praises God for our brothers the Sun, Wind, Air, Clouds, Fire, and for our sisters the Moon, the Stars, the Waters, the Earth, and every mortal human body. Saint Francis is very conscious of this brotherhood and sisterhood of all living creatures. . . .

If you travel in India, and if you are a Westerner, you are at once struck by the fact that wild animals and birds are not afraid of you, as they are, for the most part, in the Western world. In India they are on familiar terms with human beings. This is because Indians have a reverent consideration for the life of non-human living creatures. This is particularly strong in one Indian sect, the Jains. This Indian attitude toward living creatures does give the Westerner reason to think. Is not the Western attitude toward non-human living creatures too possessive, too exploiting an attitude?

Live for Understanding

I have said that we should live in order to love, and I do think that love should be the first call on every human being, but I have mentioned other things to live for. One of them was understanding and another was creating. Man seems to be unique among living creatures on this planet in having con-

Two Impressions

I am an old man, already past the allotted three score and ten and, as the old do, I quite often wake up in the night, half out of my body, so that I see between the sheets the old battered carcass I shall soon be leaving for good, and in the distance a glow in the sky, the lights of Augustine's City of God. Let me, in conclusion, pass on to you two extraordinarily sharp impressions which accompany this condition. The first is of the incredible beauty of our earth, its colors and shapes and smells and creatures; of the enchantment of human love and companionship, of human work and the fulfillment of human procreation. The second, a certainty surpassing all words and thought, that as an infinitesimal particle of God's creation I am a participant in his purposes which are loving, not malign, creative, not destructive, orderly, not chaotic and in that certainty a great peace and a great joy.

Malcolm Muggeridge, *Vital Speeches of the Day*, December 1, 1975.

sciousness and reason, and therefore having the power of making deliberate choices, and we need to use these specifically human faculties in order to direct our love right. It is so difficult to know how to apportion our love, and to decide what objects should have priority, that conscious reasoned thought is needed for this. I think, also, that using, cultivating, and developing our human reason is all the more important because even our human nature is only very partially rational. We human beings, like non-human living creatures, are governed partly by emotions and by unconscious motives. Our human reason is only on the surface of the psyche. The subconscious depths below it are unfathomable. Our unconscious motives may be good or evil. We need to bring them up to consciousness, so far as we can, and to look at them closely, in order to see whether they are good or bad and to choose and follow the good and reject the bad. There again, we need to keep our reason and our consciousness at work. A human being's life is a constant struggle between the rational and the irrational side of human nature. We are always trying to conquer a bit more of our nature for reason from blind emotion, and we are often losing ground, and then the irrational gains on the rational. As I see it, the whole of human life is a struggle to keep the reason uppermost.

Live for Creativity

Finally, we should live for being creative. What do I mean by creative? I mean trying to change this universe in which we find ourselves placed—trying to add good things to it, if possible. The universe, in the state in which we find it when we wake up to consciousness, is obviously imperfect and unsatisfactory. Many living creatures prey on each other. All animals live either on other animals which they kill in order to eat, or on vegetation, and, apart from living creatures, inanimate nature, when it is unmodified and uncontrolled, can be extremely inimical, not only to human life, but to all kinds of life. I am thinking of the earthquakes, the floods, the droughts, the storms, and the tornadoes that may destroy hundreds of thousands of lives and wreck the works of man. This, too, is an imperfection in the universe. So we should strive to add to the universe by supplementing the natural environment in which we find ourselves and partially replacing it by a man-made environment. Here, however, we have to be cautious. Since our ancestors became human, since we awoke to consciousness, we have been working on the natural environment and changing it. We have been domesticating plants and animals, instead of gathering wild plants and hunting wild animals for food. We have been constructing buildings which are not part of the non-human natural environment; we have been building great engineering works. In the nonmaterial spiritual side of life, we have been creating works of science and of architecture and of art which have a value for us in themselves. We do this creative work from disinterested motives, not from immediate utilitarian motives, yet this kind of work often turns out to have undesigned and unexpected practical uses.

I have now answered the question: 'What should man live for?' In my belief, love, creation, and understanding are the purposes for which man should live, for which he should give his life, and for which he should sacrifice himself if, in pursuit of these objects, sacrifice turns out to be demanded of him.

For Further Discussion

Chapter 1

1. M. Scott Peck writes that it is often painful to seek the truth about ourselves. Yet, he challenges us to continue on the path of self-examination and to consider the pain as "relatively unimportant" compared to finding the truth. However, earlier in his viewpoint, Peck assumes that we should avoid pain. His argument is built on the reasoning that if we have a bad "map" for our lives, we will suffer. Thus, Peck tells us to avoid one type of pain and to accept another type of pain. What is the difference between the two types of pain?

2. Plato tells the story of the cave in order to challenge his readers to escape the limitations of their present level of knowledge. However, some people might be discouraged by the cave story. As they consider the obstacles which hinder them from finding truth, they might conclude that the effort is hopeless. In what ways can Plato's image of the cave be viewed as optimistic or pessimistic?

3. Sam Keen and Anne Valley-Fox assume that myths are very important. When we study history and literature, we are studying stories about nations, groups, and individuals. When we go to family reunions or study our genealogy, we are learning about stories which are more directly connected to our lives. However, we often view ourselves as lone individuals constructing our own stories without the help of others. How can myths or stories unite groups of people (nations or families)? How can myths or stories separate people?

4. M. Scott Peck uses the image of a map, Plato uses the image of a cave, and Sam Keen and Anne Valley-Fox use the image of myths or stories. Can you develop a similar metaphor to help people better understand their lives? Explain the strengths and weaknesses of your metaphor.

Chapter 2

1. Richard Robinson rejects the existence of God. For this reason he concludes that we must create our own purpose in life. However, should we act alone and create a unique purpose for ourselves, or should we work as a team with others as we seek a common meaning in life?

2. Charles W. Colson describes a very private moment in his life when he discovered God's presence. Yet, if you read the rest of Colson's book, *Born Again*, he does not keep his experience a

private matter. He becomes involved in many religious activities. In recent years, Colson has served as a religious spokesman in debates about prison reform, the death penalty, and other social issues. In what sense is religion a private experience? In what sense is religion social?

3. Imagine conversing with Riane Eisler. On what issues would you agree with Eisler? On what issues would you modify or contradict her position? How does Eisler view the future of humanity? How do you view the future of humanity?

4. Imagine a radio talk show where both Emil Brunner and Brooke Medicine Eagle are interviewed. Where would they agree with each other and where would they disagree? How would they discuss God, spirituality, sin, redemption, and love?

Chapter 3

1. Louis Finkelstein gives a list of basic beliefs held by Jews. Corliss Lamont (at the end of the chapter) gives a list of basic beliefs held by humanists. Discuss those points where the two authors agree and disagree. Issues to consider are: the supernatural, democracy, social justice and equal opportunity, and respect for others.

2. Imagine Donald E. Miller and Bob George at a dinner table. How would they talk about politics, the Bible, salvation, the nature of God, and miracles? In what areas would they find agreement? In what areas would they disagree?

3. Imagine a chart with three columns. At the top of the three columns you list Islam, Hinduism, and Buddhism. Running down the side of the chart are a list of categories which you develop yourself (such as: salvation, spiritual reality, sin and guilt, wisdom for living, the ultimate reality behind the world, and the ultimate goal of life). How do the three religions compare to each other? How do they contrast?

Chapter 4

1. Robert Ringer wants us to "look out for number one." Paul Brownback warns that we should not love ourselves. Given these two positions, how would each author respond to Jesus' statement, "For everyone who exalts himself will be humbled, and he who humbles himself will be exalted" (Luke14: 11, NIV)? How would each author respond to Niccolo Machiavelli's warning (in chapter 5) that we must constantly be on guard to protect ourselves because everyone around us is selfish and untrustworthy?

2. Both Joseph Fletcher and C.S. Lewis reject the idea that lists of rules should dominate our lives. Both have been influenced by the Christian ideal of love. However, they disagree on other points. For example, how would Lewis respond to Fletcher's emphasis on rationality? How would Fletcher respond to Lewis' emphasis on submission to God?

3. In the first viewpoint of this chapter, Ringer writes that we should reject traditional values and think rationally. In contrast, James Q. Wilson writes that evolution has given us certain values which are part of our human nature. Thus, Ringer assumes that we are free to choose our values, and Wilson assumes that we are not free to choose our values. Who is right? Are they both right, but in different ways? Compare your thoughts with the statements made by Frank R. Zindler. He proposes that values are based in part on genetics and in part on rational choice.

4. Fred E. Katz warns that if humans simply "mind their own business," they might contribute to the evil in our world. Do you agree? If so, what positive guidance would you give to help people avoid this danger?

Chapter 5

1. Thomas Jefferson gives very specific direction to his nephew about living a good life (high moral standards, a good education, and physical health). If you were to write a letter to someone you loved, what guidance would you give for living a good life?

2. Ole Hallesby is very different from Niccolo Machiavelli. Hallesby assumes that humans are constantly seeking meaning and truth through religion. Machiavelli assumes that humans are constantly seeking power and prestige through politics. Is there a common root underlying these very different patterns of human behavior?

3. The viewpoint by Benjamin Franklin is focused on his private life. The viewpoint by Arnold Toynbee is focused on all of humanity and on the grand sweep of history. What is the relationship between our private lives and our public lives? Do we need to solve our private struggles before we can help the world? Or should we start by working on social problems, hoping that later our private struggles will be resolved? Or should we work on both levels simultaneously?

Bibliography of Books

Reading the full texts from which the viewpoints in this anthology were taken is highly recommended. In addition to those texts, the following works and websites are recommended for further study.

Books

Peter Angeles, ed.   *Critiques of God*. Buffalo, New York: Prometheus, 1976. Seventeen prominent people present a variety of arguments against belief in God.

Gleason L. Archer   *Encyclopedia of Bible Difficulties*. Grand Rapids, Michigan: Zondervan, 1982. This single volume is unique because it analyzes those stories or passages in the Bible which have caused confusion in many people's minds.

Robert O. Ballou, ed.   *The Portable World Bible*. New York: Penguin, 1976. A collection of sacred writings from the major religions of the world.

Erick C. Barret and David Fisher, eds.   *Scientists Who Believe*. Chicago: Moody, 1984. Twenty-one scientists present their arguments for believing in God.

Phillip L. Berman, ed.   *The Courage of Conviction*. New York: Ballantine, 1986. Thirty-three prominent people reveal their beliefs and how they act on them.

Emil Brunner   *Man in Revolt: A Christian Anthropology*. Translated by Olive Wyon. Philadelphia: Westminster Press, 1939. This is an in-depth study of human nature from a Christian perspective.

Emil Brunner   *The Scandal of Christianity*. Richmond, Virginia: John Knox, 1965. This short book surveys basic Christian teachings and explains tensions between Christianity and current Western thought.

Clifton Fadiman, ed.   *Living Philosophies*. New York: Doubleday, 1990. Thirty-six eminent men and women express their ultimate beliefs and doubts.

Viktor E. Frankl   *Man's Search for Meaning*. New York: Pocket Books, 1957. Frankl is a psychiatrist who survived Hitler's death camps. From his own experiences and the experiences of others, Frankl developed a type of psychotherapy. He writes that a fundamental part of every human is a longing for meaning and purpose in their lives.

Bob George	*Classic Christianity*. Eugene, Oregon: Harvest House, 1989. This is an easy to read survey of Christian beliefs.
Paul Hilberg	*Perpetrators, Victims, Bystanders: The Jewish Catastrophe 1933–1945*. New York: HarperCollins, 1992. This book studies the various roles people played in the Holocaust. The author draws the readers into the complexity of this great evil.
Arnold D. Hunt, Robert B. Crotty, and Marie T. Crotty, eds.	*Ethics of World Religions*. San Diego, California: Greenhaven, 1991. An examination of what various world religions say about ethical issues facing people today.
Paul Kurtz	*Humanist Manifesto I* (1933), *Humanistic Manifesto II* (1973), and *A Secular Humanist Declaration* (1980). Buffalo, New York: Prometheus. These are short statements of humanist beliefs.
C.S. Lewis	*The Abolition of Man*. New York: Macmillan, 1947. Despite what relativists have said about morals in this century, Lewis believes that all humans share a common moral awareness.
C.S. Lewis	*God in the Dock: Essays on Theology and Ethics*. Grand Rapids, Michigan: Eerdmans, 1994. This is a thought provoking collection of essays. Lewis was one of the best defenders of orthodox Christianity in the twentieth century.
John Lyden	*Enduring Issues in Religion*. San Diego, California: Greenhaven, 1995. A collection of religious texts and contemporary statements about religion.
Troy Wilson Organ	*The Hindu Quest for the Perfection of Man*. Athens, Ohio: Ohio University Press, 1970. This is a detailed introduction into Hinduism.
Reuben Osborn	*Humanism and Moral Theory*. Buffalo, New York: Prometheus, 1970. This is a detailed discussion of ethics from a humanist perspective.
J.B. Phillips	*Your God Is Too Small*. New York: Macmillan, 1961. Phillips suggests that most people do not understand the true nature of God. If they truly understood God, Phillips believes that they would be more open to religion.
Richard L. Purtill	*Thinking about Ethics*. Englewood Cliffs, New Jersey: Prentice-Hall, 1976. There are many helpful introductory textbooks into the field of ethics. This work is short, insightful, and fairly easy to read.

Carl Sagan

The Demon-Haunted World: Science as a Candle in the Dark. New York: Random House, 1995. Carl Sagan, a scientist and popular level author, explains how science, despite its limitations, is the best means for humans to understand themselves and the world.

Mark R. Schmidt, ed.

Human Nature: Opposing Viewpoints. San Diego, California: Greenhaven, 1999. A comparison of the ways in which Western writers have defined what it means to be human.

John Snelling

The Buddhist Handbook. Rochester, Vermont: Inner Traditions, 1991. A comprehensive and nonsectarian survey of Buddhist teaching, practice, schools, and history.

Paul Tournier

The Meaning of Persons. New York: Harper and Row, 1957. Tournier attempts to help us understand ourselves by weaving together the insights of Freud and Jung, the discoveries of biology and medicine, and ideas from Christianity.

Arnold Toynbee

An Historian's Approach to Religion. 2nd ed. New York: Oxford, 1979. After years of study of world civilizations, Toynbee surveys what he has learned about the nature of religion.

John F. Walvoord and Roy Zuck, eds.

The Bible Knowledge Commentary. Wheaton, Illinois: Victor/Scripture Press, 1983 (New Testament Volume) and 1985 (Old Testament Volume). These two volumes serve both the average reader and the more dedicated researcher by explaining the teachings of the Bible and by giving helpful background material.

Simone Weil

The Need for Roots. Translated by Arthur Wills. New York: Harper and Row, 1952. The first part of Weil's book is an interesting exploration into the basic social, emotional, and ethical needs of all humans. After her discussion of the needs of humanity, Weil considers the kind of future society we should build.

Paul Winters, ed.

Islam. San Diego, California: 1995. A collection of opposing viewpoints examining controversial issues related to the Islamic faith.

Websites from which to begin research

Atheism

americanatheist.org. A beginning point for the study of atheism.

Buddhism

tricycle.com. A site sponsored by *Tricycle* magazine, which promotes Buddhism in the U.S.

Christianity	ChristianityToday.com. This site is sponsored by *Christianity Today* magazine. It has a wide range of topics and links from a Protestant perspective.
	Catholicism.about.com. This site is an introduction into Christianity from a Roman Catholic prespective.
Ecofeminism	ecofem.org. This site has general information on ways to unify feminism and ecology.
Ethics	josephsoninstitute.org. This is a secular, non-partisan organization dedicated to cultivating the study and practice of "principled reasoning and ethical decision making."
Hinduism	hinduwebsite.com. A general information website about Hinduism.
Humanism	humanist.net. This site has many articles and links for the study of humanism.
Islam	beconvinced.com. This site gives a great deal of information about the Islam faith.
Judaism	JewishAmerica.com. A general site for learning about the Jewish faith.

Index

223